A Note From Rick Renner

I am on a personal quest to see a "revival of the Bible" so people can establish their lives on a firm foundation that will stand strong and endure the test when the end-time storm winds begin to intensify.

In order to experience a revival of the Bible in your personal life, it is important to take time each day to read, receive, and apply its truths to your life. James tells us that if we will continue in the perfect law of liberty — refusing to be forgetful hearers but determined to be doers — we will be blessed in our ways. As you watch or listen to the programs in this series and work through this corresponding study guide, I trust that you will search the Scriptures and allow the Holy Spirit to help you hear something new from God's Word that applies specifically to your life. I encourage you to be a doer of the Word that He reveals to you. Whatever the cost, I assure you — it will be worth it.

> **Thy words were found, and I did eat them;
> and thy word was unto me the joy and rejoicing of mine heart:
> for I am called by thy name, O Lord God of hosts.**
> **— Jeremiah 15:16**

Your brother and friend in Jesus Christ,

Rick Renner

Unless otherwise indicated, all scripture quotations are taken from the *King James Version* of the Bible.

Scripture quotations marked (*AMPC*) are taken from the *Amplified® Bible*. Copyright © 1954, 1958, 1962, 1964, 1965, 1987 by The Lockman Foundation. Used by permission. **www.Lockman.org**.

Scripture quotations taken from the New American Standard Bible® (*NASB*) copyright © 1960, 1962, 1963, 1968, 1971, 1972, 1973, 1975, 1977, 1995 by The Lockman Foundation. Used by permission. **www.Lockman.org**.

Scripture quotations marked (*NLT*) are taken from the Holy Bible, *New Living Translation*, copyright © 1996, 2004, 2015 by Tyndale House Foundation. Used by permission of Tyndale House Publishers, Inc., Carol Stream, Illinois 60188. All rights reserved.

Scripture quotations marked (*NKJV*) are taken from the *New King James Version®*. Copyright © 1982 by Thomas Nelson. Used by permission. All rights reserved.

Scripture quotations marked (*TLB*) are taken from *The Living Bible* copyright © 1971. Used by permission of Tyndale House Publishers, Inc., Carol Stream, Illinois 60188. All rights reserved.

Christmas — The Rest of the Story

Copyright © 2022 by Rick Renner
1814 W. Tacoma St.
Broken Arrow, OK 74012

Published by Rick Renner Ministries
www.renner.org

ISBN 13: 978-1-68031-627-8

eBook ISBN 13: 978-1-68031-665-0

Illustration and artwork by Lev Kaplan, www.kaplan-art.de. Copyright © 2020, 2021, 2022 by Rick Renner Ministries, Inc. All rights reserved.

All rights reserved. No portion of this book may be reproduced or transmitted in any form or by any means — electronic, mechanical, photocopy, recording, scanning, or other — except for brief quotations in critical reviews or articles, without the prior written permission of the Publisher.

How To Use This Study Guide

This fifteen-lesson study guide corresponds to *"Christmas — The Rest of the Story" With Rick Renner* (Renner TV). Each lesson in this study guide covers a topic that is addressed during the program series, with questions and references supplied to draw you deeper into your own private study of the Scriptures on this subject.

To derive the most benefit from this study guide, consider the following:

First, watch or listen to the program prior to working through the corresponding lesson in this guide. (Programs can also be viewed at **renner.org** by clicking on the Media/Archives links or on our Renner Ministries YouTube channel.)

Second, take the time to look up the scriptures included in each lesson. Prayerfully consider their application to your own life.

Third, use a journal or notebook to make note of your answers to each lesson's Study Questions and Practical Application challenges.

Fourth, invest specific time in prayer and in the Word of God to consult with the Holy Spirit. Write down the scriptures or insights He reveals to you.

Finally, take action! Whatever the Lord tells you to do according to His Word, do it.

For added insights on this subject, it is recommended that you obtain Rick Renner's book *Christmas — The Rest of the Story*. You may also select from Rick's other available resources by placing your order at **renner.org** or by calling 1-800-742-5593.

LESSON 1

TOPIC
A Miraculous Place in Bethlehem

SCRIPTURES
1. **Matthew 13:55,56** — Is not this the carpenter's son? is not his mother called Mary? and his brethren, James, and Joses [Joseph], and Simon, and Judas [Jude]? And his sisters, are they not all with us?....
2. **Acts 16:31** — And they said, Believe on the Lord Jesus Christ, and thou shalt be saved, and thy house.
3. **Luke 2:19** — But Mary kept all these things, and pondered them in her heart

SYNOPSIS
The 15 lessons in this study, **Christmas — The Rest of the Story**, will focus on the following topics:

- A Miraculous Place in Bethlehem
- Why Did God Choose Mary?
- Why Did God Choose Joseph?
- What Are Swaddling Clothes and What Is a Manger?
- A Holy Moment
- Who Were the Shepherds Keeping Watch?
- What Is a 'Multitude of the Heavenly Host'?
- Jesus' Baby Dedication in the Temple
- Who Were Simeon and Anna?
- Who Was Herod the Great and What Was His Relevance to the Birth of Christ?
- Who Were the Magi?
- Why Was Herod Troubled by the News of Jesus?
- What Was the Value of the Magi's Gifts?

- The Flight Into Egypt and the Massacre of the Innocents
- The Real Purpose of Christmas

More than likely, you have heard or read the Christmas story and how Jesus was born to Mary and Joseph in the little town of Bethlehem, but how much do you really know about what happened that holy night? If your understanding is based on greeting-card illustrations, chances are there are many details about Christ's birth and the events surrounding it that you've never heard. That's the purpose for this amazing study. So, if you're ready, let's begin our fascinating journey to discover *Christmas — The Rest of the Story*.

The emphasis of this lesson:

The place of Jesus' birth was not a wooden barn, but a stone cave in the city of Bethlehem. Today, the Church of the Nativity memorializes this sacred space, and it has been receiving worshipers for over 1,500 years. Mary kept a meticulous record of the events surrounding Christ's birth and served as the primary source for all the gospel writers.

Jesus Was Born in a Cave, Not in a Wooden Barn

Today, if you travel to the ancient city of Bethlehem, you will discover the historic Church of the Nativity. It draws visitors from all around the world and marks the site where Mary gave birth to Jesus, the Son of God. Now, at first glance, you would see that the site looks nothing like the traditional barn seen on typical Christmas cards. To the surprise of many, this place where the angels directed the shepherds — and where they came to worship Jesus that glorious night — is a small cave in which animals were once kept.

How do we know that this is the authentic site of Christ's birth? The earliest record confirming the location was written by Justin Martyr, the great Christian apologist who was born in 100 AD and raised about 30 miles from Bethlehem. Interestingly, throughout his growing years, he had heard stories from local residents about the place where Jesus was born. Consequently, in 150 AD, he wrote:

> "When the child [Christ] was born in Bethlehem, since Joseph could not find a lodging in that village, he took up his quarters

in a certain cave near the village; and while they were there Mary brought forth the Christ and placed him in a manger...."[1]

In addition to these words from Justin Martyr, we also have the words of the early Greek theologian and scholar Origen who in 248 AD wrote:

"...There is shown at Bethlehem the cave where He [Christ] was born, and the manger in the cave where He was wrapped in swaddling-clothes. And this sight is greatly talked of in surrounding places...."[2]

Although most of us have been raised to believe that Jesus was born in a wooden barn and placed in a wooden manger, that is not the case. If that were true, a wooden manger would not have lasted 250 years. It would have been broken down by the elements, fallen into shambles, and been discarded.

The fact is all around the city of Bethlehem there are caves, and many of them were once used as barns. In that region where wood is scarce, caves were perfectly adapted for barns. History reveals that shepherds would take a piece of rock — usually a part of the cave itself — and they would hollow it out and use it for a feeding trough, or *manger*. This explains why 250 years after Jesus' birth Origen documented that people were still coming to the cave in Bethlehem to see the "manger" where Christ was laid.

Furthermore, if you study the writings of Josephus, probably the greatest Jewish historian to ever live, you will see he wrote that there were many caves around the city of Bethlehem that shepherds used as barns. And not only did shepherds use them, but also travelers when the local inns were so full that there was nowhere else for them to sleep. These caves were great for staying warm, dry, and sleeping through the night.

The Church of the Nativity

Under Emperor Constantine, who reigned from 306 to 337 AD, Christianity became widely accepted and the persecution of Christians greatly diminished. Constantine's mother — Helena — converted to Christ and became a dedicated follower of Jesus throughout her lifetime. With the blessing of her son and the financial backing of the empire, Helena traveled to the land of Israel, which was then called Palestine, and began conducting interviews with many people who had descended from First

Century believers. Her mission was to identify and preserve the historic sites pertinent to the life of Jesus and then build a memorial on each location to safeguard it for future generations. In addition to documenting the places where Jesus was baptized and buried, Helena also determined the actual site of His birth. Indeed, the cave beneath the Church of the Nativity was determined to be the actual place where Christ was born over 2,000 years ago.

With resources provided by her son, Emperor Constantine, Helena authorized the construction of the first official Church of the Nativity in 326 AD, erecting it right on top of the renowned cave in Bethlehem where Christ was born. This first establishment was a small wooden church decorated with marble and other precious ornaments. Years later, Emperor Justinian decided to improve the memorial by building a more substantial structure. Upon its completion in 520 AD, the second Church of the Nativity was officially consecrated, and it is the cathedral that is still there today.

Remarkably, more than 1,500 years later, the Church of the Nativity still stands in Bethlehem, and people have been worshiping there ever since its opening! In fact, it's the longest continuous site of worship in the history of Christianity. Although the church and the cave have undergone numerous modifications and embellishments over the years, Jesus' birthplace can still be reached today by a flight of stairs that leads from the cathedral's main floor to the cave below. The traditional spot of His nativity is marked by a bronze star in the marble pavement. In that very spot, Mary gave birth to the Son of God so many years ago.

The Bible Documents at Least Fourteen Members of Jesus' Family

In addition to Matthew, Mark, Luke, and John, there is a treasure trove of information from Early Church writers on Jesus, His mother Mary, and His relatives. In fact, some of these facts are repeated so frequently that we know these things confidently. For example, we know Jesus' grandfather on Joseph's side was Jacob (*see* Matthew 1:16), and His grandparents on Mary's side were Joachim and Anna — Mary's father and mother, which we'll learn more about in our next lesson.

What do we know from Scripture about Jesus' family? Well, we know about Jesus' cousins — on Mary's side of the family — named Zacharias and Elizabeth. They had a son named John, who came to be known as John the Baptist; he too was Jesus' cousin (*see* Luke 1). As far as Jesus' siblings, the Bible reveals that He had four brothers and at least two sisters. Matthew 13:55 and 56 says, "Is not this the carpenter's son? is not his mother called Mary? and his brethren, James, and Joses [Joseph], and Simon, and Judas [Jude]? And his sisters, are they not all with us?...."

So according to this passage, Jesus was the firstborn, and after His virgin birth, Mary and Joseph had at least six more children — four boys and at least two girls. In this amazing family, not only do we find Jesus, the Savior of the world, but also James who became the leader of the church in Jerusalem and wrote the book of James, and Jude who became an apostle and wrote the book of Jude. After God called Mary to be the mother of Jesus and Joseph to be His foster father, He raised up other children to bring Him glory. History reveals that the other two boys — Joseph and Simon — were involved in ministry, and Jesus' sisters were married to people in ministry. This demonstrates how God calls entire families into His service.

God Calls Whole Families

Friend, God delights in saving entire families and then partnering with them to see others saved. For example, if you look at the Old Testament, you will find that God called Noah, Noah's wife, their sons, and their sons' wives to build an ark to preserve mankind as well as a sampling of all the animals and plant life on earth.

Likewise, God called Abraham and Sarah to be the father and mother of His people, eventually giving birth to the Hebrew nation. Isaac, their son, the child God promised, was also called. He married Rebecca, who gave birth to Jacob, whose name God changed to Israel. Jacob fathered 12 sons, all of whom were called by God. Then there was Moses and his brother Aaron and their sister Miriam. God used this trio — imperfect as they were — to change the course of history, bringing deliverance to His people and establishing them as a nation.

When we come to the New Testament, we see the example of Mary and Joseph and their entire family, which were called by God to do something very special. Similarly, Jesus' cousins — Zachariah, Elizabeth, and John the Baptist, their son — were all chosen by God to fulfill His purposes. How about James and John the sons of Zebedee? These two brothers were selected by Jesus to be disciples right alongside Peter and Andrew — two more brothers called into ministry.

The list of examples continues with the apostle Paul and his family. The New Testament records Andronicus and Junia were his "kinsmen" who served as apostles in the ministry (*see* Romans 16:7). Then we have Barnabas, whose name means *son of encouragement*, along with his sister Mary and her son, John Mark (Barnabas' nephew).

Mary was a follower of Christ who owned a huge apartment in the city of Jerusalem that she opened and made available to Jesus and His disciples. This was the "upper room" where Jesus had the last supper and celebrated the first communion with His disciples. It was also the place where believers received the Holy Spirit on the Day of Pentecost. Again, Mary's son was John Mark whom we read about in Acts 15:37-41. Although initially immature, he went on to become the secretary to the apostle Peter and penned Peter's gospel, which is known today as the gospel of Mark.

The list of families God chose is endless. Although these are just a few examples, it gives us concrete evidence of how He really does call and save entire families to be a part of His family and share in the work of His Kingdom. The Renner family is another modern-day example, and your family may be an example too. Even if all your members aren't saved yet, you can claim their salvation in prayer. Acts 16:31 says, "…Believe on the Lord Jesus Christ, and thou shalt be saved, and [all] thy house."

Realize that household salvation must begin with someone, so why not you? Although this verse doesn't mean that when you get saved, everyone else in your family is automatically saved, if you'll believe on the Lord Jesus Christ, eventually, all your house will be saved, and God will extend His call to your entire family.

So, if you want your family to be saved and used by the Lord to further His Kingdom, throw up your hands in prayer and say, "Lord, here I am. You saved me, and in Your mercy, I ask You to save my family. Save my parents and my siblings, and save my children and my grandchildren, that You may receive glory, honor, and great joy. In Jesus' name. Amen!"

Mary Is the Primary Source
For the Events of Jesus' Birth

Turning our attention back to the birth of Jesus, we see that Mary experienced many events that were quite extraordinary. From Gabriel's appearance announcing Christ's birth to the prophetic words spoken over Him by Simeon and Anna to the visit of the Magi with all their lavish gifts, the Bible says, "…Mary kept all these things, and pondered them in her heart" (Luke 2:19).

Many people just read right over that verse and miss its deeper meaning. Basically, this passage is telling us that the primary source in the New Testament for the story of Jesus is Mary herself. The word "kept" in the original Greek means *to keep within oneself in order to closely guard or to accurately and carefully preserve.* The word "ponder" means *to lay in order like a person who carefully and meticulously chronicles a story.*

Mary was so impacted by the events she saw happening all around her regarding the baby boy she had just given birth to that she recorded every bit of it, chronicling it carefully and meticulously in her heart. In fact, she kept the story in such perfect order that when she was visited and interviewed by apostles and gospel writers in the latter part of her life, she was able to recall all that had taken place. They in turn wrote down the information accurately and precisely as she had chronicled and journaled it inside her heart.

This brings us to an important question: Are you keeping in your memory the things that God has done for *you*? The truth is Jesus has done so many wonderful things in your life, and it is up to you to chronicle His miracles and faithfulness in your life so that you can share them and pass them on to others. The record of His interaction in your life will let others know what He wants to do in *their* life and build *their* faith.

What if Mary had not carefully chronicled and preserved these events? We and the rest of the world would have missed out on the amazing details surrounding Jesus' birth. Aren't you grateful she "kept" and "pondered" all these things in her heart? Her efforts are the reason we have all the aspects of Jesus' life in the gospels of Matthew, Mark, Luke, and John.

Each Gospel Provides a Unique Perspective

What's interesting about the gospel accounts is that they each provide certain elements that are unique to that account. For instance, when we look at the gospel of Luke, he is the only writer that tells us about Mary and Joseph traveling to Bethlehem for the census and the delivery of baby Jesus in the cave. Likewise, only Luke includes the vivid description of the angels appearing in the night sky, giving praise and glory to God, and announcing Jesus' birth to the shepherds who then traveled to Bethlehem to worship Him.

Now, if we only had the gospel of Luke, we would have no record of the Magi from the east who followed the brilliant star that led them to Jesus so they too could worship Him and present Him with their lavish gifts. Only Matthew tells us about the Magi, and only he tells us about the series of dreams God gave Joseph that directed him to relocate to Egypt in order to protect Jesus from the murderous intentions of King Herod.

Luke's account of Jesus' birth concludes with Mary, Joseph, and Jesus returning to their home in Nazareth after His dedication day and Mary's purification at the Temple. Matthew's gospel picks up when Jesus is about two years old. That's when the Magi showed up in Jerusalem, "Saying, Where is he that is born King of the Jews?" for we've seen his star in the east, and are come to worship him" (Matthew 2:2).

To get the whole story, you have to read what both Luke and Matthew wrote — not to mention John's contribution, who is the only writer who wrote of Jesus' preexistence and distinguishes Him as "the Word made flesh." Again, all the details recorded in these gospels are right from the mouth of Mary herself, who kept all these things and pondered, or journaled, them in her heart.

In our next lesson, we will focus on the question: Why did God choose Mary? Of all the girls living at that time in history, why was Mary highly favored and purposely selected by God before the foundation of the world to give birth to Christ?

STUDY QUESTIONS

Study to shew thyself approved unto God, a workman that needeth not to be ashamed, rightly dividing the word of truth.
— 2 Timothy 2:15

1. This first lesson is packed with information on Jesus' birth and related historic facts that are very valuable and faith-building. What new details did you learn about the Church of the Nativity, the manger, Jesus' family members, and the efforts of Helena, Emperor Constantine's mother?

    - The Church of the Nativity _____
    _____
    _____
    _____

    - The manger _____
    _____
    _____
    _____

    - Helena, the mother of Emperor Constantine _____
    _____
    _____
    _____

    - Jesus' family members _____
    _____
    _____
    _____

2. When it comes to God calling entire families into His service, what examples from Scripture stand out to you most? Why are these so significant to you? In what ways has God called you and your family to serve Him?

3. God called and saved Mary, Joseph, and their entire family. What do First Timothy 2:1-4 and Second Peter 3:9 say about God's greatest desire for your unsaved family members and loved ones? (Also consider God's words in Ezekiel 33:11.)

PRACTICAL APPLICATION

> But be ye doers of the word, and not hearers only,
> deceiving your own selves.
> —James 1:22

1. Mary — the sister of Barnabas — was a believer who owned a huge apartment with an upper room in the city of Jerusalem. She opened it and made it available to Jesus and His disciples, and history was made in her home. What do you have that you could open and make available to Jesus? What resources might you offer Him to help others come to know Him better?

2. Do you have family members who aren't saved? You can claim their salvation in prayer! Acts 16:31 says, "…Believe on the Lord Jesus Christ, and thou shalt be saved, and [all] thy house." Who in your family doesn't know Jesus? Begin to pray for their salvation regularly, calling out their names to God. Ask Him to remove the spiritual blindness from their eyes (*see* 2 Corinthians 4:3-6); flood their hearts with the light of truth (*see* Ephesians 1:17,18); and give them the *measure of faith* to believe and receive Jesus as their Lord and Savior (*see* Romans 12:3).

3. Mary chronicled or journaled in her heart all the wonderful things she experienced with Jesus. How about you? Are you making note of the things that God has done for *you*? Begin to take the time to journal the many wonderful ways He has provided for you, protected you, healed you, and answered your prayers. Remembering His blessings will create an attitude of gratefulness in your heart and stir your faith to keep trusting Him to be faithful.

---

[1] Martyr, Justin. *Dialogue with Trypho.*

[2] Origen. *Against Celsus.*

* For more information on this subject, it is recommended that you obtain Rick Renner's book *Christmas — The Rest of the Story.*

LESSON 2

TOPIC
Why Did God Choose Mary?

SCRIPTURES
1. **Luke 1:26-30** — And in the sixth month the angel Gabriel was sent from God unto a city of Galilee, named Nazareth, to a virgin espoused to a man whose name was Joseph, of the house of David; and the virgin's name was Mary. And the angel came in unto her, and said, Hail, thou that art highly favoured, the Lord is with thee: blessed art thou among women. And when she saw him, she was troubled at his saying, and cast in her mind what manner of salutation this should be. And the angel said unto her, Fear not, Mary: for thou hast found favour with God.
2. **John 1:46** (*NKJV*) — ...Can anything good come out of Nazareth?...
3. **Isaiah 11:1** (*NASB*) — Then a shoot will spring from the stem of Jesse, and a Branch from his roots will bear fruit.
4. **Luke 2:4** — And Joseph also went up from Galilee, out of the city of Nazareth, into Judaea, unto the city of David, which is called Bethlehem; (because he was of the house and lineage of David).
5. **Luke 1:32** — He shall be great, and shall be called the Son of the Highest: and the Lord God shall give unto him the throne of his father David.
6. **Luke 1:69** — And hath raised up a horn of salvation for us in the house of His servant David.
7. **Romans 1:3** — Concerning his Son Jesus Christ our Lord, which was made of the seed of David according to the flesh.
8. **Luke 1:26,27** — And in the sixth month the angel Gabriel was sent from God unto a city of Galilee, named Nazareth, to a virgin espoused to a man whose name was Joseph, of the house of David; and the virgin's name was Mary.
9. **Luke 1:38** — And Mary said, Behold the handmaid of the Lord; be it unto me according to thy word. And the angel departed from her.

10. **Matthew 1:18** — Now the birth of Jesus Christ was on this wise: When as his mother Mary was espoused to Joseph, before they came together, she was found with child of the Holy Ghost.
11. **Isaiah 7:14** — Therefore the Lord himself shall give you a sign; Behold, a virgin shall conceive, and bear a son, and shall call his name Immanuel.
12. **Luke 1:29-35, 38** — And when she saw him, she was troubled at his saying, and cast in her mind what manner of salutation this should be. And the angel said unto her, Fear not, Mary: for thou hast found favour with God. And, behold, thou shalt conceive in thy womb, and bring forth a son, and shalt call his name Jesus. He shall be great, and shall be called the Son of the Highest: and the Lord God shall give unto him the throne of his father David: And he shall reign over the house of Jacob for ever; and of his kingdom there shall be no end. Then said Mary unto the angel, How shall this be, seeing I know not a man? And the angel answered and said unto her, The Holy Ghost shall come upon thee, and the power of the Highest shall overshadow thee: therefore also that holy thing which shall be born of thee shall be called the Son of God. ...And Mary said, Behold the handmaid of the Lord; be it unto me according to thy word. And the angel departed from her.
13. **Matthew 1:18** — Now the birth of Jesus Christ was on this wise: When as his mother Mary was espoused to Joseph, before they came together, she was found with child of the Holy Ghost.

SYNOPSIS

The most detailed account of Mary and Joseph and the birth of Jesus is recorded in Luke's gospel. The Bible says, "And in the sixth month the angel Gabriel was sent from God unto a city of Galilee, named Nazareth, to a virgin espoused to a man whose name was Joseph, of the house of David; and the virgin's name was Mary. And the angel came in unto her, and said, Hail, thou that art highly favoured, the Lord is with thee: blessed art thou among women. And when she saw him, she was troubled at his saying, and cast in her mind what manner of salutation this should be. And the angel said unto her, Fear not, Mary: for thou hast found favour with God" (Luke 1:26-30).

The emphasis of this lesson:

It is no accident that God chose Mary to be Jesus' mother. She had been prepared and positioned by her parents with godly character and a heart of humility to give birth to and raise the Son of God.

What We Know About 'Nazareth'

The Scripture tells us that the angel Gabriel came to Mary when she was in the little obscure town called Nazareth. Although Nazareth is named in the New Testament, very little is known about it. In fact, even when we take into account ancient, extra-biblical sources, very little is understood about this tiny Galilean town located west of the Sea of Galilee.

What we do know is that it was a small agricultural village, and archaeological research concludes that during the time when Mary and Joseph lived there with Jesus, there were about 120 to 150 people living there. Although one historian speculates there were as many as 480 residents, it was still a very small, obscure village.

It was so far off the beaten track and separated from any main roads that no one would have gone there unless they intended to go there. This helps us better understand why Nathanial responded to his friend Philip with the question, "…Can anything good come out of Nazareth?" (John 1:46 *NKJV*)

The name *Nazareth* is derived from the Hebrew word *netzer*, which means *a shoot* or *a branch*. The reason this is so profound is because of what the prophet Isaiah wrote nearly 700 years before the birth of Christ. He said, "Then a *shoot* will spring from the stem of Jesse, and a *Branch* from his roots will bear fruit" (Isaiah 11:1 *NASB*). The word "branch" in this verse is the same Hebrew word *netzer* from which we derive the name *Nazareth*.

Scholars agree that Nazareth was so called because a branch of Jesse's family — a clan of the Davidic dynasty — had relocated and moved to Nazareth about the year 100 BC. Remember, the angel Gabriel said to Mary that her son would sit upon the throne of his father David. This prophetic declaration proved to be spot-on.

Joseph and Mary Were Descendants of David

A careful study of biblical history reveals that both Mary and Joseph were descendants of David. Concerning Joseph, Luke writes, "And Joseph also went up from Galilee, out of the city of Nazareth, into Judaea, unto the city of David, which is called Bethlehem; (because *he was of the house and lineage of David*)" (Luke 2:4). So Joseph really was of the seed of David, but in order for Jesus to be born of the seed of David, Mary also had to be in the Davidic royal lineage.

Regarding Mary, the angel Gabriel said, "He [Jesus] shall be great, and shall be called the Son of the Highest: and the Lord God shall give unto him the throne of his father David" (Luke 1:32). This verse clearly reveals that Jesus was conceived and birthed *without any male sexual involvement*. God Himself is the Father, which means Mary also was in the Davidic line. Luke 1:69 goes on to say, "And [God] hath raised up a horn of salvation for us in the house of His servant David."

Even the apostle Paul confirms Jesus' being David's descendant saying, "Concerning his Son Jesus Christ our Lord, which was made of the seed of David according to the flesh" (Romans 1:3). The only way Jesus could be "of the seed of David according to the flesh" was for Mary also to be of the lineage of David. She, too, had to have David's royal blood flowing through her veins. Thus, Jesus was born into the royal Davidic line that lived in the little obscure town of Nazareth. His genetic heritage literally made Him the King of the Jews.

The Significance of the Little-Known City of Sepphoris

Geographically, Nazareth was situated on a hill about 400 feet above a valley, and from its position, one could look and see the pristine city of Sepphoris. It was about four miles to the northwest of Nazareth and was a very important place during the time of Jesus.

When Herod the Great died, his kingdom was divided between his three sons: Herod Archelaus, Herod Philip, and Herod Antipas. History records that Herod Antipas became the tetrarch or ruler of Galilee, and shortly after this proclamation was made, Antipas declared Sepphoris as the capital of his new northern kingdom.

In order to display the splendor and opulence of a true capital city, Antipas launched an enormous campaign to give Sepphoris a total makeover. As you might imagine, he spared no expense. He embellished the city so greatly that it became the most splendid city in the Middle

East. Jewish historian Josephus tells us that Sepphoris was the largest and most beautiful city in the region.[1]

Interestingly, the city of Sepphoris rose to such prominence that Jewish leaders constructed a very beautiful and luxurious synagogue there, and it was this synagogue that became the largest center for sacred Jewish scrolls. As a matter of fact, this collection of scrolls was so extensive that after the destruction of the Temple of Jerusalem in 70 A.D., the Sanhedrin and all the theological leaders relocated to the city of Sepphoris where this extraordinary library of scrolls was housed.

Mary's Father Was a 'Scroll Scholar'

Now you may be thinking, *What's the connection between Sepphoris and Mary the mother of Jesus?* To understand the connection, we must go back and learn about Mary's earlier life. We know from early Christian writers that Mary's parent's names were Joachim and Anna, and they were very wealthy people. As benefactors, they gave much of their resources to the work of God while they were living in Jerusalem.

History reveals that Mary's father, Joachim, eventually relocated his family to Nazareth at some point in her young life, and while they lived in Nazareth, he served as the overseer of the sacred scrolls in the synagogue of the nearby town of Sepphoris. This means his life was built around a commitment to the Scriptures. He and his wife, Anna, didn't just send Mary to church (synagogue) on her own — they went also and were submerged in the Scriptures themselves.

As a scroll scholar, he was in the synagogue all the time, as that is where the scrolls were kept. Consequently, his family was involved in service to the Lord as well. Today, we might say Mary's father was a dedicated, church-going man of the Word. He and his family were in church, and their lives were built around serving God.

Mary Was Dedicated to God From Infancy

Other early Christian writings tell us that Mary's parents were older and had no children. They prayed for a long time for God to give them a child, and like Hannah, the mother of the Old Testament prophet Samuel, they had made a vow that if the Lord would give them a child, they would give that child to the Lord. Early Christian writers recorded that when Anna gave birth to Mary, she and her husband presented Mary to the Lord and dedicated her for His service. From the time she was an infant, they instilled in her that she was to be the handmaid of the Lord and to obey whatever God's will was for her life. Moreover, her parents told her she had been born into the world for a *special purpose*, and she believed it.

To help Mary grow spiritually, her parents enrolled her in a special school near the Temple in Jerusalem. It was specifically designed to train young girls in the Scriptures. Clearly, Mary's parents nurtured her in a home where God's Word was a priority, and it shaped her spiritually and made her spiritually sensitive. She was raised to believe she was to obey God. Accordingly, when God revealed His will to her through Gabriel — that she had been chosen to be the mother of the Messiah — she accepted it without deep struggle. She had been intentionally prepared by her parents and taught to serve God faithfully — explicitly obeying whatever God asked her to do.

This shows the importance of dedicating your children — and grandchildren — to the Lord. It is never too late to commit your family to the Lord's care and service. There are many churches today that have baby dedications, which are wonderful times of celebration. But if you stop to think about it, a baby dedication is really a *parent dedication*. It is a public ceremony in which parents or guardians bring their children and make a pledge before God and all that are present to raise their kids according to God's Word and His ways. Mary's life demonstrates how powerful your words and training are in the life of your kids. If you haven't done so already, dedicate them to the care and service of the Lord and begin to instill in their hearts and minds that God has a special purpose for their lives.

Mary Was the 'Handmaid of the Lord'

The Bible tells us clearly in Luke 1:26-30 that Mary was highly "favored" by God. The angel Gabriel says this twice in these five verses, indicating she had been singled out by God Himself for the purpose of giving birth to and raising the Son of the Most High. To meet the requirements of this monumental assignment, Mary had to be a *virgin*. Under the anointing of the Holy Spirit, Isaiah prophesied when he said, "Therefore the Lord himself shall give you a sign; Behold, a *virgin* shall conceive, and bear a son, and shall call his name Immanuel" (Isaiah 7:14).

Matthew confirms that Mary met this crucial qualification. He said, "Now the birth of Jesus Christ was on this wise: When as his mother Mary was espoused to Joseph, *before they came together*, she was found with child of the Holy Ghost" (Matthew 1:18). There are skeptics who say that this word *virgin* just means an unmarried girl, but that is simply wrong. The Greek word for "virgin" in this verse specifically describes a young girl that has never experienced a sexual relationship with a man — ever.

When Gabriel first appeared to Mary and told her she was favored of God, the Bible says, "…She was troubled at his saying, and cast in her mind what manner of salutation this should be" (Luke 1:29). The angel went on to say, "And, behold, thou shalt conceive in thy womb, and bring forth a son, and shalt call his name JESUS. He shall be great, and shall be called the Son of the Highest: and the Lord God shall give unto him the throne of his father David: And he shall reign over the house of Jacob for ever; and of his kingdom there shall be no end" (Luke 1:31-33).

Can you imagine what was going through Mary's mind in that moment? The Bible says, "Then said Mary unto the angel, How shall this be, seeing I know not a man?" (Luke 1:34) It's important to see that Mary didn't say, "This cannot be done." Instead, she asked, "*How* will this be done?" She didn't argue or doubt that what the heavenly visitor declared would come true. With an open heart, she simply asked how it would happen because she was a virgin.

Scripture says, "And the angel answered and said unto her, The Holy Ghost shall come upon thee, and the power of the Highest shall overshadow thee: therefore also that holy thing which shall be born of thee shall be called the Son of God. …And Mary said, Behold the handmaid of the Lord; be it unto me according to thy word. And the angel departed from her" (Luke 1:35,38). The word "handmaid" here describes *a female servant*. Thus, Mary was basically saying, "I am your servant and I'm available for whatever assignment you want to give me."

When God's divine assignment came, Mary was ready. She had been raised from infancy with the knowledge that she was a handmaid of the Lord and was willing to serve in whatever way God asked.

What Does It Mean To Be 'Espoused'?

Looking once more at Matthew 1:18, it says, "…When as his mother Mary was espoused to Joseph, before they came together, she was found with child of the Holy Ghost." The word "espoused" is actually the word "betrothed," which in modern terms would mean an *engagement*. Hence, when Mary was *engaged*, or pledged, to be married to Joseph, she became pregnant with baby Jesus.

It is important to understand that Jewish girls were traditionally eligible for "betrothal" at the age of 12. It is believed that Mary was between the ages of 12 and 14 when she became "betrothed" to Joseph. At that time, as tradition dictated, a public announcement of their marital intention was made. The man and woman then entered one year of training and preparation for marriage. This was viewed as a very serious period by the Jewish people. It was so legally binding that the only way out of a betrothal was through divorce.

During the one-year preparation time, the young girl would usually move into the home of her future in-laws, but she and her husband-to-be didn't have sexual relations. It was a *full year* of purity and preparation for a life-long commitment. They took marriage very seriously and did not rush into it. One reason marriages fail today is because people are not properly prepared for it. This was not the case with the Jews. They knew marriage was the most important relationship in life, so preparing for it had supreme importance. Marriage is serious and should *not* be rushed into quickly.

Luke 1:27 confirms what Matthew 1:18 says. It states that Mary was a "virgin" and was "espoused" to a man named Joseph. Again, that word "espoused" is a Hebrew concept that means they had made a public announcement that they were in the year of preparation and purity. It was during this time of preparation — "before they came together" — "that [Mary] was found with child, of the Holy Ghost" (Matthew 1:18).

So why did God choose Mary to be the mother of His Son? First, she descended from the house of David, which was a requirement. Second, she was presented by her parents to the Lord and dedicated as an infant to do the will of God. Third, Mary had been trained in the Scriptures and raised to serve God in whatever way He asked. As a virgin handmaid of the Lord, she was ready and willing to accept God's assignment to conceive, give birth, and raise His Son, Jesus.

In our next lesson, we will focus on the man Mary was espoused to — the man called Joseph. What was it about him that caused God to select him to be the foster father of Jesus? We will see that like Mary, Joseph was not randomly chosen, but purposefully selected to fulfill God's will regarding His Son, Jesus.

STUDY QUESTIONS

> **Study to shew thyself approved unto God, a workman that needeth not to be ashamed, rightly dividing the word of truth.**
> **— 2 Timothy 2:15**

1. More than likely, as you read through this lesson, you learned several new details you have never seen previously. Take a few moments to jot down the fascinating facts you want to remember regarding:

   - Mary _____
   _____
   _____

   - Mary's parents _____
   _____
   _____

   - The city of Nazareth _____
   _____
   _____

   - The city of Sepphoris_____
   _____
   _____

2. Mary was a vital part of Jesus's life from His conception to His resurrection. According to John 19:25-27, where was Mary in the time of Jesus' greatest testing? Who did Jesus entrust to take care of His mother after He was gone (*see* John 19:25-27)? Where does Acts 1:13,14 say Mary was just weeks after Jesus ascended into Heaven? What was the result of her being in that particular place that day (*see* Acts 2:1-4)?

3. Take what you learned in this lesson about Mary and in your own words, share why she was the young maiden God hand-picked to give birth to and raise His only begotten Son.

PRACTICAL APPLICATION

> But be ye doers of the word, and not hearers only,
> deceiving your own selves.
> —James 1:22

1. Imagine for a moment that you are Mary, and you've been chosen by God to give birth to Jesus, His Son. In light of the fact that you appear to be pregnant out of wedlock, what kinds of internal, personal thoughts and feelings might you have to work through? What kinds of challenges do you think you might have to work through initially with Joseph? How about with your family and friends?

2. Once Mary was born, her parents dedicated her completely to the service of God. They raised her to believe she had great purpose and that she was to obey God when He revealed His will. How about you? Have you dedicated your children — and grandchildren — to God? Are you instilling in them the fact that they have a unique purpose, and that God has a holy plan for their life? Is your life an example of what it means to be God's servant and follow Him passionately?

3. Nothing in God's plan is coincidental or accidental — everything is done on purpose, for a purpose. This means for you to be used by God, you must *cooperate* with the Holy Spirit to prepare yourself. What do you believe and understand God is asking you to do to bring Him glory and advance His Kingdom? How are you preparing for it? How are you preparing and training your children to do God's will?

---

[1] Josephus. *Antiquities of the Jews.*

[*] For more information on this subject, it is recommended that you obtain Rick Renner's book *Christmas — The Rest of the Story.*

LESSON 3

TOPIC
Why Did God Choose Joseph?

SCRIPTURES

1. **Luke 2:4** — And Joseph also went up from Galilee, out of the city of Nazareth, into Judaea, unto the city of David, which is called Bethlehem; (because he was of the house and lineage of David).
2. **Matthew 13:55** — Is not this the carpenter's son? Is not his mother called Mary?...
3. **Mark 6:3** — Is not this the carpenter, the son of Mary....
4. **Ephesians 2:10** — For we are his workmanship, created in Christ Jesus....
5. **Luke 16:11** — If therefore ye have not been faithful in the unrighteous mammon, who will commit to your trust the true riches?
6. **Matthew 1:18-20** — Now the birth of Jesus Christ was on this wise: When as his mother Mary was espoused to Joseph, before they came together, she was found with child of the Holy Ghost. Then Joseph her husband, being a just man, and not willing to make her a public example, was minded to put her away privily. But while he thought on these things, behold, the angel of the Lord appeared unto him in a dream, saying, Joseph, thou son of David, fear not to take unto thee Mary thy wife; for that which is conceived in her is of the Holy Spirit.
7. **Matthew 1:24,25** (*NLT*) — When Joseph woke up, he did as the angel of the Lord commanded and took Mary as his wife. But he did not have sexual relations with her until her son was born....
8. **Matthew 2:13,14** — ...Behold, the angel of the Lord appeareth to Joseph in a dream, saying, Arise, and take the young child and his mother, and flee into Egypt, and be thou there until I bring thee word; for Herod will seek the young child to destroy him. When he arose, he took the young child and his mother by night, and departed into Egypt.
9. **Luke 2:41,42** — Now his parents went to Jerusalem every year at the feast of the Passover, and when he was twelve years old, they went up to Jerusalem after the custom of the feast.

SYNOPSIS

As we saw in Lesson 2, Mary was highly favored by God and chosen to be the mother of Jesus. Likewise, Joseph was purposely selected by God to be Jesus' foster father. Although there were numerous other young, Jewish men God could have picked, He tapped Joseph to fulfill the role. So what was it about this young man that attracted God's attention? What can we learn from Scripture and Early Church writings that demonstrate he was the right man for such an assignment?

The emphasis of this lesson:

Being the foster father of Jesus, the Son of God, was not a position just anyone could fill. It required just the right person — someone kind, humble, faithful, successful, spiritually attuned to the voice of God, and quick to obey. Joseph was that man.

Joseph Was of the Lineage of David

One of the reasons God chose Joseph to be the earthly father of Jesus was because of his connection to David. As we saw in Lesson 2, the Bible says, "And Joseph also went up from Galilee, out of the city of Nazareth, into Judaea, unto the city of David, which is called Bethlehem; (because he was of the house and lineage of David)" (Luke 2:4). Although Mary was impregnated by the Holy Spirit and Joseph was not a genetic contributor to the formation of Jesus' life, *positionally* his heritage linked him to David and made him a prime candidate to raise Jesus.

As we saw in our last lesson, a clan of the Davidic dynasty had relocated and moved to Nazareth about the year 100 BC. The word Nazareth is derived from the Hebrew word *netzer*, which describes *a shoot* or *a branch*. Thus, there was a "branch" of David's family living in Nazareth in the First Century, and Joseph was among them. Isaiah prophesied that the Messiah would indeed be "a shoot" that would "…spring from the stem of Jesse, and a *Branch* from his roots will bear fruit" (Isaiah 11:1 *NASB*). The word "branch" in this verse is the same Hebrew word *netzer* from which we derive the name *Nazareth*.

Joseph Was a Highly Skilled 'Technician'

When most people read Matthew 13:55, which says that Jesus was "the carpenter's son," they erroneously think that Joseph was poor, but that doesn't line up with historical facts or the context of the Greek in this verse. The Greek word for "carpenter" here is *tekton*, which is where we get the word *technology*. The word *tekton* describes *a person that is highly advanced in whatever skill he possessed*. It depicts *one who makes exquisite furniture, jewelry, mosaics, stonework*, or even *one who is a building supervisor*. Thus, the word "carpenter" is a very limiting, poor translation of the word *tekton*.

As a *tekton* — translated here as "carpenter" — Joseph was highly advanced in the technical skills he possessed. He was not just a simple carpenter that worked with wood. Rather, he was a highly paid professional. Furthermore, this word *tekton* pictures one who had the expertise to envision and create with his hands a well-wrought finished product.

The word *tekton* is so connected to the idea of creativity that it was used by some ancient writers to depict literally giants or poets who produced masterful literature and poetry. Importantly, this word *tekton* was also used to describe one who could create wonders out of matter or who could manipulate materials in a marvelous way that surpassed ordinary technical skills. So when the Bible says Joseph was a "carpenter" (*tekton*), it is saying he was a high-level craftsman with amazing skills.

Joseph Was Highly Paid

The fact that Joseph was a sought-after artisan means he was also generously compensated for his work. These masterful technicians created such things as elaborate frescos painted on walls, magnificent mosaics that covered floors, sculptures carved from marble, and luxurious pieces of jewelry fashioned from gold or silver and then adorned with precious jewels. They used ivory in jewelry and furniture making, and the furnishings they designed were extravagantly embellished with ornate elements of bronze, silver, and gold and then decorated with precious jewels.

Interestingly, one scholar has noted that a *tekton* was so highly skilled that he could create shiny and splendid things whose extraordinary beauty almost made them appear to come to life. Hence, the principal meaning of a *tekton* was *one who was highly advanced and skilled; a versatile craftsman or artisan who had the technical skills to create wonders out of matter in ways that had never been seen before.*

Jesus Was Also a *Tekton*

It's likely you've heard the old saying, "like father, like son." Well just as Joseph was a *tekton* (carpenter), so was Jesus. When the people of Nazareth heard Him teach, they said, "Is not this the *carpenter*, the son of Mary…" (Mark 6:3). The word "carpenter" here is again the Greek word *tekton*, and it describes Jesus before He began His ministry. It's also important to note that they called Jesus "the carpenter," attaching a definite article. This means He wasn't just any carpenter — He was viewed as *the best carpenter in the city of Nazareth*. He had a reputation for being able to create shiny, splendid things that seemed to come to life!

Isn't that amazing! Both Joseph and Jesus are called *tektons*. They were masterful artisans who possessed the ability to mentally envision what others could not see and then create with their hands a fabulous, finished product. Just imagine: Jesus was serving as an apprentice at His father's side, learning to manipulate materials in marvelous ways and create wonders with extraordinary beauty.

If you think about it, Jesus is still doing the same thing today. As a master artisan at His Heavenly Father's side, He continues to create masterpieces out of ordinary people. The apostle Paul captures this concept clearly in Ephesians 2:10, where he wrote, "For we are his workmanship, created in Christ Jesus…."

The word "workmanship" is a translation of the Greek word *poiema*, which describes *a poet who expresses his fullest creativity when he composes and writes*. It pictures something artfully created by one who possesses the extraordinary ability to write or illustrate a masterpiece. The use of this word in Ephesians 2:10 tells us that the day we got saved, Jesus Christ — the Great Artisan — released all His creative genius to make us into something shiny and splendid! He recreated us so wonderfully that people just stand in awe of what we've become. That's what the Bible means when it says we are His *workmanship*.

'Carpenters' Were Also Masterful Stoneworkers

There's still another meaning of this word *tekton* (carpenter). It was also used to depict *a master stonemason, a masterful stone carver*, or *an architect who is engaged to architecturally design or construct a monumental building or temple fashioned of stone.* These craftsmen could take stones and cut them so that they would fit snuggly alongside one another.

Again, this description in the natural also applies to Jesus and should come as no surprise to us. According to First Peter 2:5, we are *living stones* that Jesus is cutting, sanding, and shaping as He builds us up into God's spiritual house. He is a master stonemason.

Additionally, this word *tekton*, which is wrongly translated as "carpenter" in Matthew 13:55, also depicted *the chief overseer who directed other builders and other artisans in a massive building project.* We could even call him *a building supervisor,* and people like Joseph who possessed such skills were highly compensated. When we come to the very bottom of the list of what the word *tekton* means, we find it can also indicate a *woodworking carpenter.*

Taking together all the facts we know, in all probability, Joseph was a highly advanced masterful artisan, not a woodworking carpenter. The fact is that there wasn't much wood in the region with which to work. There was, however, an abundance of stone, and knowing that the nearby city of Sepphoris was being totally renovated and embellished by Herod Antipas to become his capital city, it seems very likely that Joseph was working there.

To carry out the exquisite work being done in Sepphoris, which became known as the "ornament of Galilee," there was a need for masterful artisans. What's interesting is that most of the workers in Sepphoris lived in nearby towns such as Nazareth, which was only about four miles away. More than likely, Joseph was one of these "carpenters" (*tektons*) who worked in Sepphoris while living in Nazareth.

These *tektons* were specialists who could architecturally design and construct monumental buildings, temples, villas, and palaces. Likewise, they were also well trained to create sculptures carved from marble and impressive stone capitals that gracefully sat atop columns. Moreover, they crafted floors designed and inlaid with magnificent mosaics and walls covered with outstanding frescoes. Some *tektons* fashioned ostentatious furnishings made of bronze, silver, and gold, veneered with ivory, and adorned with precious stones.

This is who Joseph was — an extraordinary masterful artisan who had already gained a great reputation for himself even at his young age. Most scholars believe he was probably a building supervisor or some other extremely proficient craftsman with enormous authority. In any case, he was highly skilled, greatly appreciated, and abundantly compensated for what he did.

Joseph Qualified To Be Entrusted With *True Riches*

In Luke 16:11, Jesus said, "If therefore ye have not been faithful in the unrighteous mammon, who will commit to your trust the true riches?" Apparently, God had been watching Joseph and had seen how faithful he had been with the skills, resources, and finances that had been entrusted to him. His actions proved that he was responsible and ready to be entrusted with "true riches." Specifically, God knew Joseph was a man who could be entrusted with the raising of His Son, Jesus.

Think about it. If God was going to give someone the greatest assignment that had ever been given in the human race — the responsibility of raising the Son of God — would He give it to someone poor and unsuccessful? Or would He entrust the task to a reliable, successful individual that had proven themselves to be trustworthy again and again? The answer is rather obvious.

In the same way that God was watching Joseph, He is also watching *you*. The question is, what has He observed from your actions? Do you stick with projects even when things become difficult? Have you proven yourself to be a person of integrity? Can God trust you with a bigger assignment? For Joseph, the answer to these questions was a resounding *yes*.

Joseph Proved To Be *Merciful*

In addition to being trustworthy, Joseph also demonstrated great mercy. Matthew 1:18 says, "Now the birth of Jesus Christ was on this wise: When as his mother Mary was espoused to Joseph, before they came together, she was found with child of the Holy Ghost." As we saw in the last lesson, the word "espoused" describes the Hebrew *betrothal* process. Joseph and Mary had announced their engagement and were "espoused" to each other. According to Jewish custom, couples were engaged for one year. During that year, preparation for marriage took place, and sexual purity was required.

It was during this year of preparation that Mary would have relocated from Sephorris to Nazareth to live with Joseph's parents. The fact that

Joseph remained sexually pure showed him to be a man of integrity. Remaining sexually pure was viewed as a way of showing God that they were serious about having His blessing on their lives. At the end of that year, they were to be joined officially and sexually. However, it was during this time of separation and preparation that Mary became supernaturally pregnant with Jesus.

The way in which Joseph handled this unexpected situation revealed what kind of man he was. Matthew 1:19 says, "Then Joseph her husband, being a just man, and not willing to make her a public example, was minded to put her away privily." The words "just man" mean a *righteous man*. When Joseph discovered Mary was pregnant before they had come together sexually, it could have been hurtful to Joseph's honor. But he didn't want to make her a public example, so he decided to put her away privately. In other words, he did not want Mary to suffer humiliation and public embarrassment. He truly loved her and cared more about her than his own reputation. This revealed how kind and humane Joseph was.

Given the fact that Joseph was "espoused" to Mary, he had the "legal right" to put her away publicly/divorce her — and he could have even required her to be stoned for becoming pregnant before marriage. However, he decided to take the route of kindness and mercy rather than a legalistic approach. This means Joseph — a man who loved God's Word and was very committed to Scripture — was not religiously mean and legalistic. He was just the kind of man God desired to be the foster father of His Son.

Joseph Was *Spiritually Attuned* and *Obedient* to God

Another important facet of Joseph's character is revealed in Matthew 1:20, which says, "But while he thought on these things, behold, the angel of the Lord appeared unto him in a dream, saying, Joseph, thou son of David, fear not to take unto thee Mary thy wife; for that which is conceived in her is of the Holy Ghost." Amazingly, even amid an extremely difficult situation, Joseph's heart was so spiritually attuned that he could hear God speak. God needed a man of this caliber to raise Jesus — one that was spiritually attuned and who would respond to His leading.

Not only was Joseph able to hear God's voice, but he was also *obedient* to God's voice. Matthew 1:24 and 25 (NLT) says, "When Joseph woke up, he did as the angel of the Lord commanded and took Mary as his wife. But he did not have sexual relations with her until her son was born...."

Once Joseph heard from the Lord, he did not hesitate but quickly obeyed what he was told to do. This tells us that obeying God was not new in Joseph's life. The first time God asks someone to do something hard, it is usually a struggle to obey. Obviously, Joseph had been previously tested before being chosen for this assignment — and his past obedience qualified him for the task. Over time, he had developed a pattern of obedience. God knew Joseph would obey His directives, which is another reason He knew He could entrust Joseph with the responsibility of helping to raise Jesus.

Joseph's Actions Displayed *Deep Trust in God*

Shortly after Jesus' birth, the Bible says, "…The angel of the Lord appeareth to Joseph in a dream, saying, Arise, and take the young child and his mother, and flee into Egypt, and be thou there until I bring thee word; for Herod will seek the young child to destroy him. When he arose, he took the young child and his mother by night, and departed into Egypt" (Matthew 2:13,14). This act of obedience was extremely significant.

Joseph had been working very hard and had proven himself to be an outstanding man of integrity. By this time he had built a reputation in the city of Sephorris as a highly skilled professional (*tekton*), and he was earning a good income. Nevertheless, he was quick to obey when God spoke to him.

Egypt was very different from Israel. Joseph had no contacts or a permit to work. To leave and go to Egypt was a drastic, life-changing move into a pagan environment. It meant leaving all the comforts and security of what he and Mary had known and starting over from scratch. As difficult and undesirable as this move seemed to be, Joseph didn't argue with God. Instead, He promptly obeyed, demonstrating that his obedience to God was far more important than his hard-earned status.

Joseph knew he was to obey God regardless of the cost. God would be faithful to provide for their needs. In fact, this helps us see why the Lord brought unexpected gifts of gold, frankincense, and myrrh to Jesus and His family just before their trip to Egypt (*see* Matthew 2:11-15).

How about you? What does your level of obedience reveal about you? Does God know you will do whatever He asks you to do? Or does He know you will drag your heels and argue with what He asks of you? The honest answer to these questions will reveal whether or not you are ready for God's next assignment.

Joseph Was a *Solid Spiritual Leader* for His Family

Consistency is very important when you're a parent. Joseph was well aware of this, and it showed. Luke 2:41 and 42 says, "Now his parents went to Jerusalem every year at the feast of the Passover. And when he was twelve years old, they went up to Jerusalem after the custom of the feast."

Notice it says Joseph took his family *every year* to celebrate the Passover. This shows that he was very consistent in leading his family spiritually, which is a father's responsibility. Joseph didn't send his kids to church while he stayed home. He led them spiritually, and he did so by example.

Without question, God's selection of Joseph to be Jesus' foster father was not an accident, nor was it the result of a random choice. He had watched Joseph for quite a long time, and He knew all these things about his character. God had seen Joseph was trustworthy with his talents, his business, and his money. He had watched him be merciful instead of judgmental. He knew Joseph was the spiritual leader in his family and was spiritually tuned to the voice of His Spirit. Joseph had a track record of prompt obedience and was willing to sacrifice everything to do what God asked.

Friend, just as God had His eyes on Joseph, He has His eyes on you. He is studying you to see if you are being faithful to what He has already asked you to do. Are you walking in integrity — doing what is right even when no one is around? Are you merciful and humane or legalistic and judgmental? Are you leading your family spiritually and by example? Do you take them to church regularly and go yourself, or do you simply drop them off? Do you show that serving God is an option or that it is serious business? The bottom line: what good things can God say about you? If you're falling short, don't feel condemned. Receive God's conviction, repent of any wrong, and start working to make things right today.

STUDY QUESTIONS

> Study to shew thyself approved unto God, a workman that needeth not to be ashamed, rightly dividing the word of truth.
> — 2 Timothy 2:15

1. When you first read and heard that Joseph was a "carpenter," what did you think that meant? Now that you have read and heard the original Greek meaning of the word *tekton* (carpenter), how has your perspective of Joseph's occupation changed? How does this word *tekton* affect your perspective of Jesus, who is also called a "carpenter"?
2. Prior to this lesson, you probably had a mental image or idea of who Joseph was and why God chose him to be Jesus' foster father. How has your understanding of Joseph's character and God's reasons for selecting him been expanded? What do you now see that you didn't see before?

PRACTICAL APPLICATION

> But be ye doers of the word, and not hearers only, deceiving your own selves.
> —James 1:22

1. Joseph developed a pattern of *prompt obedience*, and God took note of it. What does your level of obedience reveal about you? Is it possible that God is not asking you to do anything new because you've not done what He's asked you to do in the past? What action steps do you need His strength for in order to move beyond where you are?
2. One of the most important things you can do is be a good *spiritual leader* in your home. When God looks at your life, what does He see? Does He see a strong, spiritual leader who cares spiritually for his family or someone who has abandoned their leadership role in order to be their child's best friend? Are you leading your children and spouse in word only or by example? Are you showing that serving God is an *option* or *essential* to experiencing the abundant life He has planned?
3. Just as God chose Mary and Joseph on purpose, for His purpose, He has also chosen *you* for His purpose. Get quiet and still in God's presence, and humbly ask Him this question: *Lord, why me? Why did you choose me to be a part of Your plan? What do You see in my character, my abilities, and my heart that has caused You to include me in your purposes?*

LESSON 4

TOPIC
What Are Swaddling Clothes and What Is a Manger?

SCRIPTURES

1. **Luke 2:7** — And she brought forth her firstborn son, and wrapped him in swaddling clothes, and laid him in a manger; because there was no room for them in the inn.
2. **Luke 2:1,3-7** — And it came to pass in those days, that there went out a decree from Caesar Augustus, that all the world should be taxed. ...And all went to be taxed, everyone into his own city. And Joseph also went up from Galilee, out of the city of Nazareth, into Judaea, unto the city of David, which is called Bethlehem; (because he was of the house and lineage of David): to be taxed with Mary his espoused wife, being great with child. And so it was, that, while they were there, the days were accomplished that she should be delivered. And she brought forth her firstborn son, and wrapped him in swaddling clothes, and laid him in a manger; because there was no room for them in the inn.
3. **John 6:41** — [Jesus said] ...I am the bread which came down from heaven.
4. **John 1:29,35,36** — The next day John seeth Jesus coming unto him, and saith, Behold the Lamb of God, which taketh away the sin of the world. ...Again the next day after John stood, and two of his disciples; and looking upon Jesus as he walked, he saith, Behold the Lamb of God!
5. **1 Peter 1:19** (*NLT*) — ...Christ, the sinless, spotless Lamb of God.
6. **Revelation 5:12** — ...Worthy is the Lamb that was slain to receive power, and riches, and wisdom, and strength, and honour, and glory, and blessing.
7. **Revelation 13:8** — And all that dwell upon the earth shall worship him, whose names are not written in the book of life of the Lamb slain from the foundation of the world.

SYNOPSIS

In Lesson 1, we learned about Helena, the mother of Emperor Constantine, who converted to Christ and became a devoted follower. Driven with a passion to honor the Lord and having access to the imperial treasury in Constantinople, Helena traveled to Palestine, which is what the Holy Land was called in those days, and she began to research and identify all the key locations specific to the life of Jesus.

At that time, there were still descendants of the First Century believers living in the region, so she took time to interview them and find out where the historic and miraculous events of Jesus took place. Amazingly, she discovered the location of His baptism in the Jordan River, the hill where He was crucified, and the tomb where He was buried. Using money from the imperial treasury, she constructed memorials at each site to commemorate those sacred places.

One holy site Helena determined through her interviews was the actual place of Jesus' birth, which was a cave in the city of Bethlehem. This location had been written about by Justin Martyr in 150 AD and documented again by the great theologian and scholar Origen in 248 AD. Martyr authenticated the site 150 years after Jesus' birth, and Origen confirmed it nearly 250 years after His birth. Hence, there was a great deal of information concerning Christ's birthplace, and when Helena confirmed the cave as the official site, she used funds from the imperial treasury in accordance with a decree from her son, Emperor Constantine, to begin construction of the first Church of the Nativity in 326 AD. The church was completed and dedicated 13 years later in 339 AD.

For nearly 200 years, Helena's memorial to the birthplace of Jesus stood firm. Then when Emperor Justinian came to power and saw for himself how momentous the site was, he initiated a new effort to build an even greater church on the same location. This second Church of the Nativity constructed by Justinian was completed and dedicated in 520 AD and is what you will see when you go to Bethlehem today. Thus, for more than 1,500 years, believers have been going to this sacred place to see where Jesus was born.

In the fullness of time, the Bible says Mary "…brought forth her firstborn son, and wrapped him in swaddling clothes, and laid him in a manger; because there was no room for them in the inn" (Luke 2:7). Every year around Christmastime, millions of people sing the familiar carol "Away in a Manger," but most of them don't really know what a manger is. So just what is a *manger*? What are *swaddling clothes*? And was the night of Jesus' birth really a "silent night"? The answer to these questions will likely surprise you and inspire your faith in new ways.

The emphasis of this lesson:

The manger where Jesus was laid and the swaddling clothes in which He was wrapped are quite different than what you may understand them to be. They speak of the humility of His birth and prophetically foretell God's purpose for His life.

The Roman Government 'Decreed' a Census

Everything in Scripture is included for a purpose — every person and every place has meaning. The city of Bethlehem is no exception. As we look at Luke's gospel, it says, "And it came to pass in those days, that there went out a decree from Caesar Augustus, that all the world should be taxed" (Luke 2:1). Please notice some important key words in this verse.

First, the word "decree" is the Greek word *dogma*, and it describes *a public degree*, which in this context was issued by the Roman Senate. Whenever the Roman Senate issued a "decree," it was to be obeyed with no questions asked. This empirical order was sent to "all the world." The word "world" here is the Greek word *oikoumene*, which described *the inhabited or civilized world* and depicted *the entire Roman Empire*. During the time of Caesar Augustus, the territory of the Roman Empire nearly doubled in size. Consequently, they needed more money to expand and improve the empire's infrastructure.

The purpose for the decree was "…that all the world should be taxed" (Luke 2:1). In Greek, the word "taxed" means *to be enrolled*. It was a word used to describe *an empire-wide "census" to determine the population of the empire and to determine the possible tax revenue and budget of the government*. A census of this nature was done very rarely.

The Bible specifically says the "decree" for this census was given by "Caesar Augustus." Caesar Augustus was *Octavian*; he succeeded Julius Caesar and was responsible for the deaths of Mark Antony and Cleopatra — two historical figures that were friends of Herod the Great.

Scripture then says, "And this taxing was first made when Cyrenius was governor of Syria" (Luke 2:2). There are some critics of Scripture who claim that there is no evidence of a world-wide census when Cyrenius was governor of Syria, but that is not true. They miss the fact that Cyrenius was governor during *two separate time frames*, and in one of them a census was indeed decreed.

The Whole World Was on the Move

Luke continues his narrative by saying, "And all went to be taxed, every one into his own city" (Luke 2:3). Notice the word "all." It is the Greek word *pantes*, and it means *everyone; all; no one excluded*. Also notice the words "every one"— the Greek word *hekastos*. Similarly, it means *everyone; all; no one excluded*. Twice in the same verse, we are told that *everyone, all,* and *no one excluded* went into his own city to be counted in the census. This means everyone in the entire Roman Empire was on the move trying to get back to where the roots of their family first began.

Just imagine the hustle and bustle that abounded in those days. It was the first time in human history that an entire empire was moving at the same time. To accommodate the Roman decree, scads of businesses, schools, and stores were closed. Salaries were suspended and work was brought to a screeching halt as individuals and whole families from across the Roman world were packing their belongings and hitting the road to return to the town of their family lineage to be registered in the census.

Although the abundance of travelers was great for generating tourism revenue, it was extremely inconvenient and difficult for scores of people. More than likely, the concert of complaining against the government was at an all-time high. "Why can't we just stay where we are for this census?" people likely moaned. Nevertheless, God was clearly at work orchestrating events to fulfill biblical prophecy.

Think about it. More than 730 years before Christ was born, the prophet Micah predicted that He — the One who would rule Israel — would come forth from Bethlehem (*see* Micah 5:2). In order for that prophecy to be fulfilled, God put the entire world in movement to get Mary and Joseph to Bethlehem at the time of Jesus' birth. And the census decree from Augustus Caesar was the catalyst that brought it about.

This demonstrates that *God will do anything necessary to get you where you need to be*. He will even inconvenience people and change their plans to fulfill His plan and the destiny for your life.

The Little Town of Bethlehem

Our story continues in Luke 2:4, where Luke writes, "And Joseph also went up from Galilee, out of the city of Nazareth, into Judaea, unto the city of David, which is called Bethlehem; (because he was of the house and lineage of David)." When the Bible says, "Joseph went up," it is literally referring to the elevation of Jerusalem, which is higher than the city of Nazareth.

This journey that Joseph and Mary set out on was long and difficult for anyone, much less a woman who was nine months pregnant and ready to give birth at any moment. The distance from Nazareth to Bethlehem is 70-90 miles, depending on the route. For a person in good shape, traveling an average of 20 miles a day, the trip would normally take about 4 days. But for a very pregnant woman like Mary, it would take 7 to 10 days. She would need multiple breaks along the way to rest and use the restroom. They would also have to set up and break down camp numerous times.

Clearly, there was nothing "easy" about this trip. Yet, God was orchestrating His plan to get Mary and Joseph to Bethlehem at the time of her delivery so that Christ could be born there as it was prophesied. Therefore, not only will God inconvenience people and change their plans in order to fulfill His plan, but He will also inconvenience *you* and change *your* plans in order to get you where you need to be to fulfill your destiny.

Just because something is difficult or inconvenient doesn't mean it is not of God. The Cross and the scourging were horrific, yet they were a part of God's plan to redeem man through Jesus Christ. As you serve God, there will be hard things you will need to do to get to where you need to be. But if you're willing and obedient, God will supernaturally empower you to do whatever you need to do to fulfill His purposes in your life. That is what Joseph and Mary were committed to doing. They were willing to obey God, and God got them where they needed to be — the little town of Bethlehem.

Interestingly, the name "Bethlehem" means *house of bread*. In John's gospel, Jesus stated repeatedly and in various ways, "…I am the *bread* which came down from heaven" (John 6:41). Thus, Jesus is the Living Bread that came down from Heaven and was born in Bethlehem, the *house of bread*. With pinpoint precision, God fulfilled His prophecy through Micah and supernaturally birthed spiritual nourishment for the entire world in the form of His Son. Jesus is the bread of salvation, the bread of healing, the bread of peace, and the bread of all of God's promises.

Jesus Was the 'Firstborn' of Several Children

Joseph obeyed the Roman decree and arrived in Bethlehem, "to be taxed with Mary his espoused wife, being great with child. And so it was, that, while they were there, the days were accomplished that she should be delivered" (Luke 2:5,6). When the Bible says Mary was "great with child," it means s*he was very pregnant or very far along in a pregnancy.*

Then it happened! The miracle occurred that still has people celebrating and worshiping God all over the world more than 2,000 years later. The Bible says, "And she brought forth her firstborn son, and wrapped him in swaddling clothes, and laid him in a manger; because there was no room for them in the inn" (Luke 2:7).

Notice that Jesus is called Mary's "firstborn." This is the Greek word *prototokos*, which means *firstborn* and indicates *the first of other children*. There are some religious faiths that teach Mary only had one child — Jesus. However, that's not what the Bible teaches. The fact that Jesus is called the "firstborn" denotes other children were born after Him, and Matthew 13:55 and 56 confirm this. As we saw in Lesson 1, their names were James, Joseph, Simon, and Jude — along with at least two sisters. So after Jesus' birth, Mary and Joseph had at least six additional children.

Wrapped in 'Swaddling Clothes' and Laid in a 'Manger'

Looking once more at Luke 2:7, it says once Jesus was born, Mary "...wrapped him in swaddling clothes, and laid him in a manger; because there was no room for them in the inn." The phrase "wrapped in swaddling clothes" carries a fascinating meaning. It is a translation of the Greek word *sparganoo*, which describes *the bandages or strips of material used for wrapping the little legs of newborn lambs.*

There were animals all around Jesus the night He was born — most likely little lambs and a shepherd or two among them. That being the case, these bandages or strips of material (swaddling clothes) would have been available in the cave where Christ was born. Thus, the strips of cloth that were normally used to wrap and protect the legs of baby lambs were used by Mary to wrap up baby Jesus — *the Lamb of God!*

Isn't that amazing! Jesus' first appearance on earth symbolically foreshadowed His purpose for coming — to be the Lamb of God. Again and again, John the Baptist declared Jesus was "…the Lamb of God, which taketh away the sin of the world" (John 1:29; *see* also v. 36). The apostle Peter identified Christ as "…the sinless, spotless Lamb of God" (1 Peter 1:19 *NLT*). And in the book of Revelation, we see that the plan of salvation concerning Jesus — the Lamb of God — was in place "from the foundation of the world" (*see* Revelation 13:8). This signature title for our Savior is what makes the term "swaddling clothes" extremely significant.

Once wrapped up, Mary laid Jesus in a "manger." Now in the minds of most people, when they think of a manger, they imagine a small wooden structure filled with hay, which is what has appeared on countless Christmas cards through the years. But that is not what it was. The word "manger" in Luke 2:7 is the Greek word for *an animal's feeding trough.* Regarding this manger, scholar and theologian Origen wrote in 248 AD:

> **"…There is shown at Bethlehem the cave where He [Christ] was born, and the manger in the cave where He was wrapped in swaddling-clothes. And this site is still greatly talked of in surrounding places…."[1]**

Amazing! The cave in Bethlehem still had the original manger in which Christ was born nearly 250 years after His birth. Think about it: If the manger had been made of wood, it would have rotted or fallen into disrepair and been discarded. The fact is mangers in those caves were not made out of wood but of stone. They were literally carved out of the wall of the cave, which is why it was still visible hundreds of years later. Even more interesting is that when you descend the steps into the grotto below the Church of the Nativity today, there is still a manger of stone carved into the wall of the cave. Whether it's the original manger or not, we don't know. In any case, it would have been a manger just like the one Mary used.

Why Was There 'No Room in the Inn'?

Religious tradition says that the reason Mary and Joseph ended up in the cave with the animals is because they were too poor to pay for a room. However, that is not true. Joseph was a highly compensated masterful artisan (*tekton*). The reason there was no room in Bethlehem for them to stay in a room was because the town was tiny, and the multitude of travelers that were crowding the city for the Roman census meant the town couldn't house everyone. By the time Joseph and Mary made it to Bethlehem, all the rooms were already taken. Retreating to the back of a cave was all that was available, and that is where Mary gave birth to the Son of God.

This brings us to another important question: Was the night Jesus was born really a "silent night"? Probably not. The reality is, there are random caves all across the Judean countryside, and this particular cave in Bethlehem was normally used as a place of refuge for shepherds and their flocks. More than likely, it was filled with noisy animals, possibly a few shepherds, and even weary travelers who also couldn't find a place to stay. Thus, the night that Jesus was born was anything but *silent*. In fact, it was downright *noisy*.

The cave in which Jesus was born is the one located just below the present-day Church of the Nativity in Bethlehem. As we noted, it can be reached by descending a flight of stairs from the cathedral's main level. Today, a bronze star on the marble floor marks the place of that sacred space where the incarnation took place. This fact has been well-documented by Christian writers from the earliest of times, and there is no reason to doubt it.

In our next lesson, we will take a closer look at the details of the miracle that occurred that holy night.

STUDY QUESTIONS

Study to shew thyself approved unto God, a workman that needeth not to be ashamed, rightly dividing the word of truth.
— 2 Timothy 2:15

1. What is your greatest takeaway regarding the historic worldwide census decreed by the Roman Senate and Caesar Augustus? What

new insights did you learn about Joseph and Mary's long journey to the town of Bethlehem?
2. When you hear that Jesus, the Son of God, was born in a noisy cave that was normally used as a refuge for shepherds and their flocks, how does this change the way you see the Christmas story?
3. One of the most amazing facts about the cave beneath the Church of the Nativity is that it has been well-documented by Early Church Fathers since the Second Century as the authentic site of Jesus' birth and it's still visible today. How does this knowledge influence and shape your faith?

PRACTICAL APPLICATION

> But be ye doers of the word, and not hearers only,
> deceiving your own selves.
> —James 1:22

1. People around the world celebrate Christmas in unique ways. How do you and your family celebrate Christmas? What are some of the traditions that you have established in your home? How have you learned to keep Jesus at the center of the celebration and not get drowned out by all the commercialism?
2. The Bible says that when Jesus was born, He was wrapped in "swaddling clothes," which describe *the bandages or strips of material used for wrapping the little legs of newborn lambs.* Jesus' first appearance on earth — as *the Lamb of God* — symbolically prophesied His purpose for coming. Carefully read Isaiah's description of the Lamb of God in Isaiah 53:3-7. When you see Jesus as your *personal,* sacrificial Lamb, how does it touch your heart? (Consider First Peter 1:18-21.)?

---

[1] Origen. *Against Celsus.*

* For more information on this subject, it is recommended that you obtain Rick Renner's book *Christmas — The Rest of the Story.*

LESSON 5

TOPIC
A Holy Moment

SCRIPTURES

1. **John 3:19** — And this is the condemnation, that light is come into the world, and men loved darkness rather than light, because their deeds were evil.
2. **John 1:1,3** — In the beginning was the Word, and the Word was with God, and the Word was God. …All things were made by him; and without him was not any thing made that was made.
3. **Colossians 1:16** — For by him [Jesus] were all things created, that are in heaven, and that are in earth, visible and invisible, whether they be thrones, or dominions, or principalities, or powers: all things were created by him, and for him.
4. **John 1:10** — He was in the world, and the world was made by him, and the world knew him not.
5. **John 1:14** — And the Word was made flesh, and dwelt among us….
6. **Philippians 2:6-7** — Who, being in the form of God, thought it not robbery to be equal with God: but made himself of no reputation, and took upon him the form of a servant, and was made in the likeness of men.
7. **Luke 1:38** — And Mary said, Behold the handmaid of the Lord; be it unto me according to thy word….
8. **Hebrews 4:15,16** — For we have not an high priest which cannot be touched with the feeling of our infirmities; but was in all points tempted like as we are, yet without sin. Let us therefore come boldly unto the throne of grace, that we may obtain mercy, and find grace to help in time of need.
9. **Philippians 2:8** — And being found in fashion as a man, he [Jesus] humbled himself, and became obedient unto death, even the death of the cross.
10. **Philippians 2:5** — Let this mind be in you, which was also in Christ Jesus.

SYNOPSIS

As we noted in previous lessons, the grotto beneath the Church of the Nativity in Bethlehem is the indisputable site where Jesus was born. The earliest historical records confirm this to be true. Apologist and philosopher Justin Martyr, who died in 165 AD, said that Mary and Joseph, "being unable to find lodging in the town, they sought shelter in a cave of Bethlehem."[1] Equipped with such knowledge, Emperor Constantine's mother — Helena — conducted numerous interviews with descendants of First Century believers and confirmed the cave to be Christ's birthplace. Accordingly, she converted it into a small church and embellished it with marble and other precious ornaments. Years later, in 520 AD, Emperor Justinian erected an even greater church on the same site.

Although the cave and the church have undergone numerous restorations and modifications, the birthplace can still be reached today by a flight of stairs that leads from the cathedral's main floor to the cave below. The traditional spot of Jesus' birth is marked by a bronze star in the marble pavement. Amazingly, in that very spot, the Creator of all we can and cannot see clothed Himself in human flesh and began to live among us for a brief time. That is what the word "incarnation" means — *God in the flesh*. And that is the miracle that took place that holy night.

The emphasis of this lesson:

The *incarnation* — God clothing Himself in human flesh and taking on the physical form and likeness of man in the person of Jesus — is the miracle of Christmas.

Jesus Is the Light of the World and God in the Flesh

The apostle John — the disciple who personally knew Jesus more intimately than any other disciple — made an extraordinary statement about Jesus that no one else made. He said, "In him was life; and the life was the *light* of men. And the *light* shineth in the darkness; and the darkness comprehended it not" (John 1:4,5). Essentially, John is declaring that despite how dismal and evil the darkness of this world is, it can not overcome or put out the light of Jesus Christ!

Jesus Himself declared that He indeed is the "…light [that] is come into the world…" (John 3:19). The early Greek theologian and scholar Origen carried this truth forward and in 248 AD wrote, "The people who sat in darkness [the Gentiles] saw a great *Light*."[2] Jesus — the Light of the world — was born in that barn-like cave in Bethlehem over 2,000 years ago.

Ever since then, believers have been celebrating that miraculous holy moment when God Almighty laid aside His glory to appear temporarily on earth as a man. How wonderful and marvelous it is to think that God momentarily discarded His divine outward attributes to appear as a man in the form of Christ Jesus! This miracle is called the *incarnation* — the mystery of when God became flesh and dwelt among us. John so powerfully documented this event by saying:

> **In the beginning was the Word, and the Word was with God, and the Word was God. …And the Word was made flesh, and dwelt among us, (and we beheld his glory, the glory as of the only begotten of the Father,) full of grace and truth.**
> **— John 1:1,14**

The Early Church father Irenaeus and the council of Nicaea used the Greek word *karkousthai* to describe that divine moment when the Word became flesh in the person of Jesus Christ. Early Church fathers Jerome and Ambrose later used the Latin word *incarnatus* to describe the same moment when God took on a human form and human nature. From that time until ours, it's been referred to as the *incarnation*. This foundational Christian doctrine teaches that the divine nature of the Son of God was perfectly united with human nature in one person, Jesus — who was both fully God and fully man. That is the miracle of Christmas and what Christmas is all about.

Jesus Is God and Has Always Existed

Something else amazing took place when Jesus was born. As the animals and others moved about in that cave, they were totally unaware that their Creator had been born among them. Suddenly, they could hear a little baby crying, but they had no idea that God Himself had entered their world in the form of a small child.

Looking again at John 1:1, John declared, "In the beginning was the Word, and the Word was with God, and the Word was God." Notice the word "word" is used three times in this verse, and each time it's used, it is a reference to Christ in His pre-incarnate existence. In fact, John boldly states, "…The Word was with God." The Greek actually says, *pros ton Theon*, which means the Word — Jesus — was *face to face with God*! It depicts Jesus and the Father so close to each other that they can feel each other's breath breathing on their faces. It is a picture of divine intimacy among the members of the Godhead.

This tells us that when Jesus was born in Bethlehem, it was not His beginning — it was simply His physical manifestation in human form. Furthermore, it demonstrates that Jesus is not just a mere component or symbol of God, but in fact, *He is God*. Although some people may feel that is blasphemous to say, it is the clear truth being communicated in Scripture. *Jesus is God!* Just as the Father always existed, so also Jesus has always existed.

Jesus Is Creator-God

The apostle John goes on to say, "All things were made by him; and without him was not any thing made that was made" (John 1:3). This lets us know that not only is Jesus God, but He is also the Creator of all things. The apostle Paul reiterates this same truth in Colossians 1:16 where he wrote, "For by him [Jesus] were all things created, that are in heaven, and that are in earth, visible and invisible, whether they be thrones, or dominions, or principalities, or powers: all things were created by him, and for him."

Ironically, when Jesus was in the world among the people He created, they didn't recognize Him. John 1:10 says, "He was in the world, and the world was made by him, and the world knew him not." Yet, although the people were blinded to His true identity, creation itself knew who He was.

- When Jesus spoke to the *wind* and the *waves*, they acknowledged Him as Creator and obeyed Him (Matthew 8:26,27; Mark 4:39-41).
- When Jesus gave thanks to God and blessed the *five loaves* and *two fish*, the atomic particles of the food recognized His voice and spontaneously multiplied themselves so thousands of people could be fed (Matthew 14:15-18; Mark 6:35-44).
- When the disciples were in trouble at sea, the molecular structure of the *water* solidified in such a way that Jesus walked on top of the water (Matthew 14:22-25; Mark 6:45-50).
- When Jesus spoke to and cursed the fruitless fig tree, it discerned His voice as Creator and obeyed His command (Matthew 21:18,19; Mark 11:12-14,20,21).

Again, Jesus is the Word, "...and the Word was with God, and the Word was God. ...And the Word was made flesh, and dwelt among us..." (John 1:1,14). The word "dwelt" in this verse is a Greek word that describes *a tent or a tabernacle* and its use here literally means that Jesus' physical body became the tent that God lived in during His earthly life. Just imagine — the omnipotent Creator literally pitched a tent of human flesh in the form of Jesus Christ and tabernacled among us for 33 temporary years. Indeed, there is no god like our God!

Philippians 2:6-8 — A Remarkable Christmas Passage

In addition to Luke and John's gospels, the miraculous incarnation is also described by the apostle Paul most eloquently in Philippians 2:6-8. Although most people use these verses in connection with the crucifixion and the resurrection, it's actually one of the greatest Christmas passages in the Bible. Speaking of Jesus, Paul wrote, "Who, being in the form of God, thought it not robbery to be equal with God: but made himself of no reputation, and took upon him the form of a servant, and was made in the likeness of men" (vs. 6,7).

The first thing to notice is the opening phrase, "Who, being in the form of God...." This could literally be translated from the Greek as, *"Who, eternally existing in the form of God...."* Next, note the word "form." It is the Greek word *morphe*, and it describes *an outward form*. In Jesus' *preexistence* — before He was born as a baby in Bethlehem — He was not just a component of God, nor a symbol of God. *He was God!* As the eternal God, Jesus possessed the outward appearance as well as all the glory and power of God — a presence so strong that humans could not endure its manifestation. Therefore, He had no other choice but to re-clothe Himself with a new form so that He could physically appear and live among us.

Philippians 2:6 goes on to say that Jesus "made himself of no reputation." This phrase is the Greek word *kenoo*, which means *to make empty, to vacate, to evacuate,* or *to shed*. Because it was impossible for God to appear to man as God in all His glory, He had to change His outward form. The only way He could make this limited appearance as a Man was to willfully, deliberately, and temporarily let go of all the attributes we usually think of when we consider the characteristics of God. For 33 years on this earth,

God divested Himself of all His heavenly glory, and the Scripture says, "…[He] took upon him the form of a servant…" (Philippians 2:7).

The phrase "took upon him" is a translation of the Greek word *lambano*, which means *to seize, to grab hold of, to take to one's self,* or *to grasp*. The use of this word lets us know that God literally reached out from His eternal existence, reached into the material world He had created, and *took human flesh upon Himself.* He longed to be with us so much and bring us salvation that He emptied Himself of all His external glory and reached into the material world He created and seized human flesh and dressed Himself in it.

Specifically, the Scripture says God took upon Himself "the form of a servant." The word "form" here is again the Greek word *morphe*, which describes *an outward form*. In birth, God put on the form of man — and particularly a "servant." The word "servant" is the Greek word *doulos*, and it describes *the lowest form of a servant whose principal task is to do the bidding of his owner*. He is *to help, assist, and fulfill his master's desires and dreams to the exclusion of all else. This servant's existence was to service his master in whatever way the master asked or demanded*. It is *one whose will is completely swallowed up in the will of another*.

When Jesus came, He came as a servant of the Father to do whatever the Father asked of Him, which included His sacrificial death on the Cross. Jesus' will was completely swallowed up in the will of the Father (*see* John 5:30). And as He took on the form of a servant, the Bible also says He "…was made in the likeness of men" (Philippians 2:7).

The words "was made" describe the *miracle of Christmas* — when Jesus was literally formed in the womb of the Virgin Mary and was made a man. When Mary said to the angel Gabriel, "…Be it unto me according to thy word…" (Luke 1:38), the Holy Spirit overshadowed her in that moment, and she conceived in her womb Jesus, the Son of God. He was made in "the likeness of men." The word "likeness" refers to not only the visible, physical likeness but also the likeness of how we think and feel.

When God left His heavenly home and took upon Himself human flesh, a great supernatural exchange was made. He literally became one of us in every way. This is why Hebrews 4:15 says, "For we have not an high priest which cannot be touched with the feeling of our infirmities; but was in all points tempted like as we are, yet without sin." Friend, Jesus understands and has experienced every emotion and every temptation you have had or will ever have. He has faced it all — *yet*, He never fell into sin! That is why

God invites us to "...come boldly unto the throne of grace, that we may obtain mercy, and find grace to help in time of need" (Hebrews 4:16).

Jesus, Our King, Made a Great Exchange To Be With Us

In Philippians 2:8, the apostle Paul continued His description of the incarnation saying, "And being found in fashion as a man, he humbled himself, and became obedient unto death, even the death of the cross." The word "fashion" here is the Greek word *schema*, and it has been borrowed from a true story in ancient literature of a king who exchanged his kingly garments for a brief period of time for the clothing of a beggar. Because he was the king and dressed in royal splendor, he could not freely walk among the people. All he could do was look upon them from his balcony above. But one day he decided to take off his royal garments, disguise himself as a commoner, and make his way out of his palace and into the streets. As a result of re-clothing himself in the garb of everyone else, no one recognized him as the king. Thus, he was able to walk among the population.

All of this imagery and meaning is packed into the word *schema* — translated here as the word "fashion." This is the word the Holy Spirit prompted Paul to use to describe the birth of Jesus. God wanted to be with us greatly, but He couldn't come in His splendor and glory because it was too great for human flesh to endure. So, He re-clothed Himself to look like one of us and took on the human form of Jesus — our King. He exchanged His royal, celestial robes for the clothing of flesh and lived among us for 33 years. He loved us so much that "...he humbled himself, and became obedient unto death, even the death of the cross" (Philippians 2:8). The word "even" is the Greek word *de*, and it means *emphatically EVEN!*

Putting the meanings of all these words together, here is the *Renner Interpretive Version (RIV)* of Philippians 2:8:

> **Can you imagine it! Jesus humbled Himself to such a lowly position and became so obedient that He even stooped low enough to die the miserable death of a Cross.**

Think of it! Almighty God came to this earth as a human being in the womb of a human mother for one purpose — so that He could one day die a death on a cross to purchase our salvation!

As you celebrate Christmas, remember its real purpose, and "let this mind be in you, which was also in Christ Jesus…" (Philippians 2:5). Just as God willingly humbled Himself and did whatever He had to do to serve us, save us, and change us, we need to be willing to surrender our pride and do whatever we need to do to reach those who really need help. That's what Jesus did for us and it's what we are commanded to do for others.

In our next lesson, we'll find out exactly who the shepherds were that the angels appeared to when Jesus was born and why the angels appeared to this particular group of shepherds when there were so many other shepherds in the land of Israel.

STUDY QUESTIONS

> Study to shew thyself approved unto God, a workman that needeth not to be ashamed, rightly dividing the word of truth.
> — 2 Timothy 2:15

1. According to Matthew 13:55 and 56, Jesus had four brothers and at least two sisters. But are those *all* His brothers and sisters? To help you answer, carefully read Jesus' words in Matthew 12:48-50. (Also consider Romans 8:29.)

2. We saw in Philippians 2 that before Jesus came to earth and took upon Himself the form of a servant, He *preexisted* in the form of the eternal God. What does the apostle John say about Jesus' preexistent state in John 1:1-4? And what does the apostle Paul reveal about Him in Colossians 1:15-17? (Also consider John 17:5, 24; Micah 5:2; Hebrews 7:3.)

PRACTICAL APPLICATION

> But be ye doers of the word, and not hearers only, deceiving your own selves.
> — James 1:22

1. Jesus was the ultimate example of a *servant* of God — *one whose will is completely swallowed up in the will of the Father.* Jesus said,

"...I do not seek or consult My own will [I have no desire to do what is pleasing to Myself, My own aim, My own purpose] but only the will and pleasure of the Father Who sent Me" (John 5:30 *AMPC*). In what areas of your life are you *most* like a servant of God? Where are you *least* like a servant? In what ways can you cooperate with the Holy Spirit to cultivate this character of Christ's humility in your life?

2. When Jesus was born of Mary, He literally became like one of us in *every way* — having "...a shared feeling with our weaknesses and infirmities and liability to the assaults of temptation..." (Hebrews 4:15 *AMPC*). Yet He did *not* sin! For this reason, you are to come fearlessly, confidently, and boldly before God's throne to receive His mercy when you sin, and His grace to grow and live victoriously. Take a few moments right now to ask God for forgiveness and mercy in the areas you have failed and for His empowering grace to grow spiritually.

---

[1] Martyr, Justin. *Dialogue with the Jew Trypho.*

[2] Origen. *Against Celsus.*

* For more information on this subject, it is recommended that you obtain Rick Renner's book *Christmas — The Rest of the Story.*

LESSON 6

TOPIC

Who Were the Shepherds Keeping Watch?

SCRIPTURES

1. **Luke 2:8-12** — And there were in the same country shepherds abiding in the field, keeping watch over their flock by night. And, lo, the angel of the Lord came upon them, and the glory of the Lord shone round about them: and they were sore afraid. And the angel said unto them, Fear not: for, behold, I bring you good tidings of great joy, which shall be to all people. For unto you is born this day in the city

of David a Saviour, which is Christ the Lord. And this shall be a sign unto you; Ye shall find the babe wrapped in swaddling clothes, lying in a manger.

SYNOPSIS

On the night Jesus was born, an angel appeared to a group of shepherds to make the announcement that a Savior — Christ the Lord — had been born in the nearby city of Bethlehem. Did you ever stop and think about these shepherds and their sheep? Did you ever wonder if there was something special about them — something that made them different than all the others? There were many shepherds in Israel during that time, so was there a reason God sent an angel to this particular group of shepherds and not to others? The answer will likely surprise you!

The emphasis of this lesson:

The Bethlehem shepherds had a unique responsibility above all other shepherds: they raised the lambs to be sacrificed in the Temple. It was to these shepherds that the angel of the Lord appeared and announced Jesus' birth. The sign the angel gave to authenticate that they had found the Messiah was that He would be wrapped in swaddling clothes.

Special Shepherds With Special Sheep

Immediately after Mary delivered baby Jesus, the Bible says, "And there were in the same country shepherds abiding in the field, keeping watch over their flock by night" (Luke 2:8). What's interesting is that very near Bethlehem today, there is an ancient field called the Shepherds' Field where shepherds used to abide and keep watch over their flock day and night. There is a long-held tradition that these particular shepherds bred and raised sheep that were to be offered as lambs without blemish for temple sacrifices — especially at the time of the Passover.

The Jewish historian Josephus wrote that every year, up to 260,000 lambs were sacrificed in the Temple in Jerusalem during Passover.[1] That said, Jewish regulations required that these sacrificial lambs be birthed very near to the city so they could be easily and quickly transported to the Temple where they would be sacrificed.

For this reason, these Bethlehem Shepherds were a special group under rabbinical care who raised lambs to be used for Temple sacrifice. They were charged to maintain a clean stable for a birthing place and to work close to Bethlehem because it was only about five miles from Jerusalem. Sacrificial lambs that were to be offered to God had to be without blemish, which means they had to meet very strict religious standards. To ensure those legal requirements were met, these special shepherds bred and raised lambs in a very controlled environment.

At the time of a newborn lamb's birth, every male was inspected to assure it was without defect. Immediately after the newborn lambs were birthed, these shepherds wrapped their legs in strips of cloth or swaddling clothes to protect them from injury. The shepherds then placed the newborn lambs into a stone feeding trough — a manger — until a priest came to inspect them and declare them to be without blemish and fit to be used as sacrificial lambs.

Bethlehem's Connection to 'Migdal Eder'

The fact that Bethlehem was to be the birthplace of the Messiah was foretold by the prophet Micah, who wrote, "But thou, Bethlehem Ephratah, though thou be little among the thousands of Judah, yet out of thee shall he come forth unto me that is to be ruler in Israel; whose goings forth have been from of old, from everlasting" (Micah 5:2). The word *Ephratah* (or *Ephrathah*) seems to be the name of Bethlehem itself or of a district in which Bethlehem was situated. It is first mentioned in Scripture as the place right near where Rachel — Jacob's most cherished wife — died while giving birth to Benjamin (*see* Genesis 35:16-20). The Bible says Jacob buried her near *Ephratah* (Bethlehem) and then journeyed a short distance to Migdal Eder — or the tower of Edar (*see* Genesis 35:21).

Early Church historian Eusebius (260/265-339 AD) wrote that near Bethlehem was a place called Migdal Eder,[2] which means *the tower of the flock*. The reason this is significant is because in ancient Jewish writings, it was stated that animals found as far as Migdal Eder could be used for sacrifice in the Temple in Jerusalem. It was at this ancient tower, shepherds under rabbinical care brought their pregnant lambs to give birth to newborn lambs that were to be used in temple sacrifices in Jerusalem. Because the tower was deemed to be a clean stable for a birthing place, the shepherds stayed near the tower as they grazed their flocks night and day.

Noted historian Alfred Edersheim (1825-1889 AD), who was a Jewish convert to Christianity, said, "We know that, on the night in which our

Savior was born, the angel's message came to those who probably alone of all in or near Bethlehem were 'keeping watch.' For, close by Bethlehem, on the road to Jerusalem, was a tower, known as Migdal Eder, the 'watch-tower of the flock.' For here was the station where shepherds watched their flocks destined for sacrifices in the Temple. So well known was this, that if animals were found as far from Jerusalem as Migdal Eder, and within that circuit of every side, the males were offered as burnt-offerings, the females as peace-offerings.... It seems of the deepest significance, almost like the fulfillment of type, that those shepherds who first heard tidings of the Saviour's birth, who first listened to angels' praises, were watching flocks destined to be offered as sacrifices in the Temple."[3]

These Shepherds Were *Constantly* Watching and Guarding Their Sheep

Looking once more at Luke 2:8, it says, "And there were in the same country shepherds abiding in the field, keeping watch over their flock by night" (Luke 2:8). So, these were special shepherds in a special field watching special sheep. The Bible says they were "abiding in the field," which means they were *lodging in the fields* — fields that were very close to Bethlehem and Migdal Eder (*the tower of the flock*).

Remember, these shepherds were under rabbinical care. Their mission was to breed and raise lambs to be used for sacrifice in the Temple. They would take the pregnant lambs that were ready to give birth to this very clean and controlled environment, and once the newborn lambs were born, they wrapped their legs in swaddling clothes and laid them in the manger to be inspected by the priests.

Luke 2:8 also says these shepherds were "...keeping watch over their flock by night." In Greek, a literal translation of the words "keeping watch" would be, "they were guarding and watching," or "they were guarding and guarding." It is the very word used to describe *soldiers that are watching over what has been entrusted to their care*. It is also the word used to describe *shepherds who have an unbroken vigilance to watch over their flocks*. Furthermore, the tense here means they were *constantly guarding or constantly watching* their flocks. Again, these were special, sacrificial lambs that were to be offered at the Temple — particularly at the time of the Passover.

Suddenly, the 'Glory of the Lord Shone Round About Them'

The Bible goes on to say, "And, lo, the angel of the Lord came upon them, and the glory of the Lord shone round about them: and they were sore afraid" (Luke 2:9). First, notice the word "lo" — the Greek word *idou*. It means *bewilderment, shock, amazement,* and *wonder*. The use of this word lets us know the shepherds weren't expecting an angelic encounter. Also notice that initially only *one* angel "came upon" the shepherds. This phrase "came upon" is the Greek word *ephistemi*, which describes *a sudden and surprising, glorious appearance that takes one off guard*. Clearly, these shepherds were not sitting around waiting for an angelic appearance. Thus, the abrupt arrival caught them totally by surprise. It was a *sudden, surprising, dazzling* event.

Immediately with the angel's arrival, "…The glory of the Lord shone round about them…" (Luke 2:9). In Greek, the word "glory" is *doxa*, and it describes *the glory, splendor, and weighty presence of God — a presence so heavy that you would collapse under it*. This means when the glory of God came on these shepherds who were just minding their business, not only was it brilliant and filled with splendor, but it was also a heavy presence of God that caused these shepherds to suddenly collapse under its weight.

Luke writes that the glory of the Lord "…shone round about them…" (Luke 2:9). This phrase is a translation of the Greek word *perilampo*, which means *to shine all around* or *to encircle with light*. It depicts *a very strong beam of light* that suddenly began shining on these shepherds. There they were lying on the ground, and rather than the entire countryside being lit up, the brightness of God's glory encased the shepherds in a single beam of light — almost as if they have been singled out!

What was the shepherd's response? The Bible says, "…And they were sore afraid" (Luke 2:9). A literal translation of the words "sore afraid" in Greek would be *they feared with a great fear* or *they were seized with terrible fear*. This is why in Luke 2:10, it says the angel said, "Fear not." In Greek, "Fear not" is a very strong prohibition that literally means, "*Stop fearing, and stop it right now!*" Clearly, this angel didn't come to scare the shepherds — he came to thrill them with the best news they had ever heard.

When the Angel Announced Jesus' Birth, He Also Declared Jesus' Life Mission

Once the angel calmed their fears, he said, "...Behold, I bring you good tidings of great joy, which shall be to all people" (Luke 2:10). Interestingly, the word "behold" is again the Greek word *idou*, a word expressing *bewilderment*, *shock*, or *wonder*. In this verse, it is the equivalent of saying, "Wow! What you're about to hear is absolutely amazing!" The phrase "good tidings" is the Greek word *euangelidzo*, which describes *the greatest news anyone has ever heard*, and the words "great joy" describe *gargantuan* or *enormous joy*.

The angel then said, "For unto you is born this day in the city of David a Saviour, which is Christ the Lord" (Luke 2:11). This tells us that when the angel appeared to the shepherds, the birth had already taken place — and it occurred in the City of David, which is Bethlehem, just a stone's throw from Shepherds' Field.

Who had been born? The angel said, "...a Saviour, which is Christ the Lord" (Luke 2:11). These words were a declaration from the very beginning of who Jesus was and what His mission on earth would be.

Jesus is "Savior." The word "Savior" is the Greek word *Soter*, meaning *Deliverer*, *Savior*, *Healer*, and *Preserver*. This was a divine announcement that Jesus had come to set mankind free from the dominion of Satan's rule on earth (*see* 1 John 3:8). Thus, Jesus brought *saving* power, *delivering* power, *healing* power, and *preserving* power to those who put their trust in Him.

Jesus is also the "Christ." In Greek, "Christ" is the word *Christos*, meaning *Christ, the Anointed One*. It is the Greek equivalent for the Hebrew word *Messiah*. Thus, the angel announced that Jesus is *the Anointed One* — the long-awaited Messiah that was *anointed to deliver, to save, to heal,* and *to preserve*.

Jesus is "Lord." The word "Lord" is a translation of the Greek word *Kurios*, which is capitalized in Greek just as it is in English, and it means *Lord* or *Absolute Lord*. It is the identical word used for *Jehovah* in the Septuagint, which is the Greek version of the Old Testament. Thus, the angel declared that Jesus was *Jehovah in the flesh*, and there is no higher authority or power than Jesus Christ in all the world or all the universe. He reigns supreme!

The 'Sign' the Angel Gave Was Tailor-Made for the Shepherds

For the shepherds to know for sure that they had found Christ the Lord, the angel gave them a specific sign for which to look. He said, "And this shall be a sign unto you; Ye shall find the babe wrapped in swaddling clothes, lying in a manger" (Luke 2:12).

The word "sign" is the Greek word *semeion*, and it describes *a sign to alert a viewer as to where he is or that what he is seeing is authentic*. Moreover, it means *to document, verify, or guarantee; it is proof*. Something else that is significant in this verse are the words "unto you," which is the Greek word *humin*, and it literally means *especially for you*. Thus, the angel said, "And this shall be a verifying proof, especially for you shepherds. You will find the babe wrapped in swaddling clothes, lying in a manger." Here we see God is giving a sign to these shepherds using words and symbols He knew they would understand.

Next, notice the word "find." It is the Greek word *heurisko*, and it *usually points to a discovery made due to an investigation*. It's where we get the word *eureka*. The use of this word indicates that the shepherds would have to do some searching in order to locate Jesus.

Unless you have visited the city of Bethlehem or studied its topography, you may be unaware of just how many caves exist in the area. They are all around the hills of Bethlehem, and the shepherds during New Testament times actually lived in these grottos. It was a place for them to rest, escape the rain or intense heat, and care for their sheep.

Knowing that there were numerous caves in the area, the shepherds would need to exert effort and look diligently to "find" the Christ-child. The instant they found Him would be a euphoric moment when they would say, "Eureka! We've found Him! We've found the Savior — Christ the Lord!"

The angel said Jesus would be a "babe," which is the Greek word *brephos*, and it describes *a newborn*. Without question, the very night Jesus was born was the night the angel appeared to the shepherds, and it was probably within hours — possibly minutes — of His birth. The confirming sign that the "babe" they found was truly Christ the Lord was that He would be "wrapped in swaddling clothes."

'Swaddling Clothes' Was the Sign

We saw in our previous lesson that the phrase "wrapped in swaddling clothes" is the Greek word *sparganoo*, and it describes *bandages or strips of material used for wrapping the little legs of newborn lambs to protect them from injury*. Remember, these were shepherds under rabbinical care who were raising lambs to be used for temple sacrifice in Jerusalem. When a newborn lamb was birthed, it was customary for them to wrap the lamb in swaddling clothes. Once the sacrificial lamb was wrapped, it was then placed in a manger to be inspected by a priest to make sure it was a lamb without blemish.

In essence, the angel was telling the shepherds: "I know that your assignment is to care for the little sacrificial lambs that are born under your watch and to wrap them in swaddling clothes, but I'm announcing to you that you've had your eyes fixed on the wrong lambs. The real Lamb of God has just been born in Bethlehem. When you find Him, you'll know it's Him because He will be wrapped in swaddling clothes just like you would normally use for newborn lambs. This is a sign especially for you."

When the shepherds found Christ, they knew it was him because he was dressed in swaddling clothes, just like the angel had told them. The moment they saw Him in those strips of cloth was *a eureka moment* indeed.

The Bible tells us after they found Him, they departed and began to report the good news to anyone who would listen. The people who heard what these rabbinical shepherds had to say wondered at their words (*see* Luke 2:17,18). "These are no ordinary shepherds," the people said. "They are rabbinical shepherds who really know what they're doing. Their job is to watch over and care for sacrificial lambs, and if they say they've found the real Lamb of God, they've made an amazing discovery."

In our next lesson, we will learn about the multitude of the heavenly host that showed up the night Jesus was born.

STUDY QUESTIONS

> **Study to shew thyself approved unto God, a workman that needeth not to be ashamed, rightly dividing the word of truth.**
> — 2 Timothy 2:15

1. Jesus' earthly mission was clear from the moment He was born. Do you know what it was? Take a look at these verses from God's Word for some eye-opening insight: Matthew 5:17,18; 20:27,28; Luke 19:10; John 3:17; 10:10; 18:37; First Timothy 1:15; and First John 3:8.
2. Likely, you have heard of the shepherds watching their flocks the night that Jesus was born — and how the angels appeared to them and announced His birth. But what new things did you learn about the shepherds and the sheep of which you were unaware?

PRACTICAL APPLICATION

> But be ye doers of the word, and not hearers only, deceiving your own selves.
> — James 1:22

1. How important is telling the true story of Christmas in your family's annual celebration? If you haven't done so already, why not make this a new tradition! Why not share the story of Jesus *first* — reading it to your children and grandchildren *before* the gifts are opened? It is a great way to honor the Lord and connect your kids and grandkids closer to Jesus!
2. When the angel appeared to the Shepherds, he declared Jesus to be *Savior*, *Christ*, and *Lord*. How does the meaning of this prophetic proclamation affect you personally?
3. The Bible says when the miraculous events regarding Jesus' birth took place, "Mary kept all these things, and pondered them in her heart" (Luke 2:19). How about you? Do you have a collection of memories of how God has moved in your life — how He supernaturally protected you and provided for you? How He gave you mercy when you didn't deserve it and unexpected favor when you needed it most? Take some time now to remember how His presence has manifested in your life and to *thank Him* for His incredible goodness!

---

[1] Josephus. *The Wars of the Jews*.

[2] Eusebius. *Onomasticon*.

[3] Alfred Edersheim, *The Life and Times of Jesus the Messiah* (Grand Rapids, MI: Christian Classics Ethereal Library, 1953).

* For more information on this subject, it is recommended that you obtain Rick Renner's book *Christmas — The Rest of the Story*.

LESSON 7

TOPIC
What Is a 'Multitude of the Heavenly Host'?

SCRIPTURES

1. **Luke 2:13,14** — And suddenly there was with the angel a multitude of the heavenly host praising God, and saying, Glory to God in the highest, and on earth peace, good will toward men.
2. **1 Timothy 3:16** — ...God was manifest in the flesh, justified in the Spirit, seen of angels, preached unto the Gentiles, believed on in the world, received up into glory.
3. **2 Corinthians 4:6** — For God, who commanded the light to shine out of darkness, hath shined in our hearts, to give the light of the knowledge of the glory of God in the face of Jesus Christ.
4. **Luke 2:15,16** — And it came to pass, as the angels were gone away from them into heaven, the shepherds said one to another, Let us now go even unto Bethlehem, and see this thing which is come to pass, which the Lord hath made known unto us. And they came with haste, and found Mary, and Joseph, and the babe lying in a manger.
5. **Luke 2:12** — And this shall be a sign unto you; ye shall find the babe wrapped in swaddling clothes, lying in a manger.
6. **Luke 2:17-19** — And when they had seen it, they made known abroad the saying which was told them concerning this child. And all they that heard it wondered at those things which were told them by the shepherds. But Mary kept all these things, and pondered them in her heart.

SYNOPSIS

On the night Jesus was born, the Bible says the angel of the Lord appeared to the shepherds abiding in the fields in Bethlehem. It was a single angel that appeared in the dazzling glory of God — a glory so heavy it caused the shepherds to collapse to the ground. Suddenly, they found themselves encased in a concentrated beam of light looking up at an angel who began to announce that Christ the Savior had been born in Bethlehem.

Then something indescribable happened. Luke 2:13 and 14 says, "And suddenly there was with the angel a multitude of the heavenly host praising God, and saying, Glory to God in the highest, and on earth peace, good will toward men." Just what was this "multitude of the heavenly host"? Why did they show up? Is there something about this supernatural scene that we may have missed that is important for us to know?

The emphasis of this lesson:

The night Jesus was born, there was a supernatural manifestation of the massive angelic armies of Heaven. They came to salute their Commander-in-Chief who was just beginning His earthly assignment. Looking into the face of Jesus was the first time they could look directly into the face of God.

A Massive Manifestation of the Armies of Heaven

Once the angel of the Lord had announced the birth of Jesus and gave the shepherds the sign that would authenticate it was Him, the Bible says, "And suddenly there was with the angel a multitude of the heavenly host praising God…" (Luke 2:13). The word "suddenly" in Greek is *exaiphnes*, which means *unexpectedly* or *suddenly*. It depicts *something that takes one off guard and by surprise*. Scripture says that suddenly a "multitude of the heavenly host" appeared and filled the night sky. The word "multitude" is the Greek word *plethos*, and it describes *a massive, huge crowd; a great number*. It depicts something *colossal, enormous*, or *immense*. In this case, it was a colossal crowd of the heavenly "host." The Greek word for "host" is *stratia*, which is the term that describes *an organized group of soldiers* or *an assembly of soldiers*. In this case, *a massive assembly of Heaven's army* had shown up on the scene to witness the event. Suddenly, as far as the shepherds' eyes could see, warring angels filled the sky.

Just imagine what the shepherds saw that night. First, they were dazed by a brilliant beam of light emanating from the angel of the Lord that suddenly appeared. God's glory was so heavy they collapsed to the ground. Next, the angel announced the birth of the long-awaited Messiah in Bethlehem. Third, the shepherds went from seeing the sudden appearance of *one* angel to seeing the sudden, supernatural appearance of *a colossal crowd of Heaven's warring troops* filling the sky!

Why Would the Massive Army of Heaven Suddenly Materialize?

The answer to this question is found in First Timothy 3:16. Here, the apostle Paul was writing about the incarnation — the great mystery of when God took on human flesh. He said, "…God was manifest in the flesh, justified in the Spirit, *seen of angels*, preached unto the Gentiles, believed on the world, received up into glory."

First, note the word "manifest." It is the Greek word *phaneroo*, and it means *to appear* or *become visible*. When Jesus was born in Bethlehem, God *appeared* or was *made visible* in the flesh for the very first time. This was not His beginning; it was simply the first time He became visible. Before Christ's birth, angels had never seen the face of God, but the moment He was born, the invisible God became physically visible and "seen" by angels.

The word "seen" is a translation of the Greek word *horao*, which means *to see; to behold; to perceive;* or *to delightfully view*. It pictures *a scrutinizing look* or *to look with the intent to examine; to fully view* or *to experience*. The night Jesus was born, Jesus was "seen of angels." The sky was filled with the armies of Heaven that came to take a scrutinizing look at Jesus — enabling them to delightfully view and behold God in a way like never before!

In Old Testament times, prior to the miraculous birth of Christ, the angels had not seen or looked into the face of God — neither had any man. In Exodus 33:20, God told Moses that no man can see His face and live, because the glory of God is so powerful, no flesh can endure it. God put Moses in a cleft of the rock and covered him with His hand. Once God's presence passed, He removed His hand so Moses could see His back (*see* Exodus 33:22,23). This enabled Moses to experience God's glory and survive.

Even the angels who stand in the very presence of God cannot look directly into His face, which is why Isaiah 6:2 tells us that they cover their face with their wings. Just as a person covers his eyes to protect them from the blinding light of the midday sun, these angels use their wings to protect their eyes from looking directly into the glory of God.

So when Jesus was born as a babe in Bethlehem, for the first time ever, it was possible to see the face of God in the face of Jesus. The moment He appeared in the flesh as a human infant, the angels came in massive numbers to see Him and behold the face of God for the very first time. That is why Paul wrote, "…God was manifest in the flesh, justified in the Spirit, [and] *seen of angels…*" (1 Timothy 3:16).

You may ask, "Why was this incalculable number of angels dressed like heavenly soldiers and not just in dazzling white?" Well, they were dressed like warring soldiers because Jesus — even at His birth as an infant — was Lord of all and the Commander-in-Chief of Heaven's army. As Commander-in-Chief, He had just begun the most important assignment in the history of the world, and now the angels came dressed appropriately to salute and honor their Commander — and to look directly into the face of God for the very first time!

Friend, as a believer in Christ, you too can see the face of God! The Bible says, "For God, who commanded the light to shine out of darkness, hath shined in our hearts, to give the light of the knowledge of the glory of God in the face of Jesus Christ." (2 Corinthians 4:6). The face of Jesus reveals the face of God and His glory, and as a born-again child of God, you have the privilege of seeing and experiencing the glory of God personally (*see* 2 Corinthians 3:18).

The Angels of Heaven Repeatedly Gave Praise and Glory to God

Looking again at Luke 2:13 and 14, the Bible says, "And suddenly there was with the angel a multitude of the heavenly host praising God, and saying, Glory to God in the highest, and on earth peace, good will toward men." The word "praising" here is the Greek word *aineo*, which means *to extol*, *to exalt*, or *to praise*. And the word "saying" is a translation of the Greek word *legonton*, which means *saying* or *announcing*. Equally important here is the tense of this word, which would literally be translated *saying and saying and saying* or *announcing and announcing and announcing*.

Over and over and over again, this myriad of warrior angels was repeatedly announcing the birth of God in the flesh. He is Emmanuel — *God with us!* With one harmonious voice, Heaven's armies celebrated the birth of Jesus, saying again and again, "…Glory to God in the highest, and on earth peace, good will toward men" (Luke 2:14).

Many people say that the angels *sang* when they announced Jesus' birth, but when we look very closely at the original text, it doesn't say anything about the angels singing. Hopefully, this news doesn't disappoint you. Is it possible that part of their "praises" was singing? Maybe. But if we are true to what the passage says, there is no indication of angels singing. In fact, there's not a single verse anywhere in the Bible that says angels sing.

Of course, Scripture does record the singing of others. For instance, in Zephaniah 3:17, we find that God sings over His people. In Revelation 5:9 and 10, we read that the 24 elders in Heaven sing a new song to the Lamb of God, declaring His worthiness to open the seven-sealed scroll. Although the angels of God do many things, singing doesn't seem to be one of them according to Scripture.

What Is the Role of Angels?

A careful study of Scripture reveals that one of the main functions of angels is to listen to what God says and then speak verbatim what He has instructed them to speak. Thus, we could say that angels are *repeaters*. Interestingly, once an angel or a group of angels has delivered God's message word for word and said what He told them to say, they disappear just as quickly as they appeared. We see this happen repeatedly throughout Scripture.

Consider these examples of how these God-sent heavenly messengers work:

- The angel Gabriel announced to Zachariah that his wife, Elizabeth, would give birth to a son who was called John the Baptist (Luke 1:11-20).
- The angel Gabriel also announced the birth of Jesus to Mary (Luke 1:26-38).
- A multitude of heavenly angels appeared in the sky and announced the birth of Jesus to the group of shepherds in Bethlehem (Luke 2:9-14).
- Angels announced the resurrection of Jesus in three different gospels (Matthews 28:1-7; Mark 16:5-7; Luke 24:4-7).

- Two angels appeared to the apostles at the time of Jesus' ascension and announced that He would return in the same manner as they saw Him go into Heaven (Acts 1:10,11)
- In the coming days, the voice of the archangel will announce the rapture of the Church, declaring the moment when believers will be caught up to be with Jesus forever (1 Thessalonians 4:16,17).
- And the book of Revelation is filled with angelic announcements that initiate judgments upon the earth and its unbelieving inhabitants.

Again, the Bible says angels are "…spirit-messengers sent out to help and care for those who are to receive his salvation" (Hebrews 1:14 *TLB*). In the case of Christ's birth, the angel of the Lord delivered the announcement to the shepherds of Bethlehem and then was joined by a massive multitude of Heaven's armies who gave praise and glory to God and then vanished out of sight.

The Shepherds Were the First Evangelists

Luke goes on to say, "And it came to pass, as the angels were gone away from them into heaven, the shepherds said one to another, Let us now go even unto Bethlehem, and see this thing which is come to pass, which the Lord hath made known unto us. And they came with haste, and found Mary, and Joseph, and the babe lying in a manger" (Luke 2:15,16).

Notice the Bible says the shepherds came with *haste*, which means *to move as quickly as possible*. Indeed, they wasted no time to begin looking for the newborn Lamb of God in the city of David. The words of the angel of the Lord were still fresh in their ears: "And this shall be a sign unto you; ye shall find the babe wrapped in swaddling clothes, lying in a manger" (Luke 2:12).

The moment they made it to the cave and saw the Christ-child in the manger, the Bible says, "…They made known abroad the saying which was told them concerning this child. And all they that heard it wondered at those things which were told them by the shepherds" (Luke 2:17,18). Here we see that the shepherds were the first evangelists to preach the Good News of Jesus. They told as many people as they could about the Lamb of God that had just been born and proclaimed Him to be the Savior — Christ the Lord — just as the angel had announced to them.

Scripture says, "...All they that heard it wondered at those things, which were told them by the shepherds" (Luke 2:18). The word "wondered" here means that the hearers were *amazed, astonished, astounded, baffled, bewildered, confounded, dumbfounded, flabbergasted, at a loss of words, shocked*, and *stunned*. Again, the listeners knew that these were no ordinary shepherds. They were intelligent, well-trained shepherds under rabbinical care with the sacred assignment of watching over sheep that were to be used as sacrifices at the Temple in nearby Jerusalem. When they collectively said, "We have found the real Lamb of God, and He was wrapped in swaddling clothes just like a newborn lamb," all who heard the firsthand witnessing from the shepherds were left speechless. They took it to be a very serious announcement.

Mary Treasured It All in Her Heart

How did Mary, the mother of Jesus, respond to all that was happening? Luke 2:19 says, "But Mary kept all these things, and pondered them in her heart." As we saw previously, the word "kept" is the Greek word *suntereo*, which means *to treasure, to keep from corruption*, or *to keep a priceless possession*. Mary carefully guarded the memories of all these events inside her.

The Bible says she also "pondered them in her heart." The word "pondered" here means *to keep in perfect order*, which means Mary kept an internal journal of all these events, arranging them in chronological order. She understood that something quite special was taking place, and to the best of her ability, she kept an accurate record of it.

Years later, toward the end of her life when she was living in Ephesus under the care of the apostle John, she was visited by Luke and the other gospel writers. And because she had "pondered" all these things in her heart, keeping them in order and free of corruption, she was able to relay the pure memories to them, sharing exactly what happened concerning the events of Jesus' birth.

How about you? Do you treasure the things God has done in your life? Do you keep them as uncorrupted memories to share with others? It would be good for you to take some time to recall the amazing things God has done for you and your family. This is a life-giving, faith-building practice for you and for those with whom you share.

In our next lesson, we will look at what took place the day Mary and Joseph dedicated Jesus to God in the Temple.

STUDY QUESTIONS

Study to shew thyself approved unto God, a workman that needeth not to be ashamed, rightly dividing the word of truth.
— 2 Timothy 2:15

From the opening of God's Word in Genesis to its finale penned by John in the book of Revelation, angels have appeared all along the continuum of time, playing a significant role in God's service.

1. Of all the stories of angelic appearances in Scripture, which is one of your favorites? Why?
2. According to Hebrews 1:14, what is a primary role of angels that directly affects you?
3. Another major job angels carry out is revealed in Psalm 34:7 and 91:11,12. What is it?
4. Have you ever experienced this type of angelic involvement personally? If so, share what happened.

PRACTICAL APPLICATION

But be ye doers of the word, and not hearers only, deceiving your own selves.
— James 1:22

1. At the birth of Jesus, God spoke to the shepherds, giving them a sign *especially for them* that He knew they would understand. How does God speak to *you*? What types of things does He say and do that confirm it is Him speaking and directing your life?
2. The "multitude of the heavenly host" that suddenly materialized was *a massive army of Heaven's angels*. How do you think you would have responded had you been one of the shepherds in the field who saw and heard these warrior angels praising God that holy night?
3. How do you think the sights and sounds of that supernatural event would have impacted your relationship with God from that moment forward?
4. When you hear that the angels of Heaven showed up at Jesus' birth because they had not yet seen or looked into the face of God, what does this speak to you personally?

LESSON 8

TOPIC
Jesus' Baby Dedication in the Temple

SCRIPTURES
1. **Luke 2:21,22** — And when eight days were accomplished for the circumcising of the child, his name was called Jesus, which was so named of the angel before he was conceived in the womb. And when the days of her purification according to the law of Moses were accomplished, they brought him to Jerusalem, to present him to the Lord.
2. **Romans 12:1** — I beseech you therefore, brethren, by the mercies of God, that ye present your bodies a living sacrifice, holy, acceptable unto God, which is your reasonable service.
3. **Deuteronomy 6:5** — And thou shalt love the Lord thy God with all thine heart, and with all thy soul [mind], and with all thy might.

SYNOPSIS
Just after the birth of Jesus, while Mary and Joseph were still in Bethlehem, they had a special baby dedication for Him at the Temple in Jerusalem. The Scripture says, "…They brought him to Jerusalem, to present him to the Lord" (Luke 2:22). This was an important and powerful act of obedience on behalf of Mary and Joseph — one that demonstrates a practice we as believers are called to do in our daily Christian walk.

The emphasis of this lesson:

Just as Joseph and Mary presented Jesus to God at the Temple, we are to dedicate our children and grandchildren to God. By presenting them to the Lord, we're making a commitment to train them in the Christian faith and to instill that faith in them. A baby dedication is a picture of how God wants us to surrender our body and soul to Him daily.

What Is a Baby Dedication?
Luke wrote many details about the Christmas story and Jesus' early life that are only contained in his gospel. Jesus' baby dedication is an example.

Luke 2:21 tells us, "And when eight days were accomplished for the circumcising of the child, his name was called Jesus, which was so named of the angel before he was conceived in the womb."

About 32 days after Jesus was circumcised — 40 days after His birth — Mary and Joseph were still with Him in Bethlehem. Luke 2:22 says, "And when the days of her purification according to the law of Moses were accomplished, they brought him to Jerusalem, to present him to the Lord." What Mary and Joseph did at the Temple that day is what most of us would call a *baby dedication*.

In essence, a baby dedication is a ceremony in which believing parents, and sometimes entire families, make a commitment before the Lord to raise their child according to God's Word and God's ways. It is a pledge that provides parents an opportunity to express publicly their desire to lead and spiritually nurture their child to love and serve God. Today, baby dedications can happen privately or in front of an entire congregation so that everyone can witness the commitment being made. Either way, the parents' intent is to make a public statement that they will train their child in the Christian faith and seek to instill that faith in their son or daughter.

Even among the Jews at the time of Jesus, a baby dedication ceremony involved the reading of key Bible passages and a verbal exchange in which the parents publicly agreed to raise their child according to God's Word. Still today, there are baby dedications in synagogues, but the first baby dedication that we read about in Scripture happened with a woman named Hannah who had been barren for many years. She cried out to God and asked Him for a child. He responded and blessed her and her husband, Elkanah, with a son who was named Samuel. As promised, they dedicated Samuel to the Lord (*see* 1 Samuel 1), and he became a mighty prophet, priest, and judge in Israel for several decades.

If you think about it, a baby dedication is really more of a *parent dedication*. In that moment, when the parents or guardians stand before God and others with their child, they make a commitment that they're going to raise their son or daughter (or grandchild) according to the Word of God. They are going to take him or her to church regularly and teach that child to obey the Lord in all their ways.

Jesus' Baby Dedication

As memorable as Samuel's dedication was, the most well-known baby dedication is that of Jesus. Looking once more at Luke 2:22, it says Mary and Joseph "…brought him [Jesus] to Jerusalem, to present him to the Lord." The word "present" is the Greek word *paristemi*. It is a compound of two words: the word *para*, meaning *alongside*; and the word *istemi*, meaning *to place* or *to stand*. When these two words are compounded to form the word *paristemi*, it means *to place at one's disposal*; *to surrender*; *to offer a sacrifice to God*; *to present as a special offering to God*; or *to dedicate once and for all*.

Thus, when Mary and Joseph "presented" Jesus to the Lord, they *surrendered Him to the Lord* and *placed Him at the Lord's disposal*. Moreover, they symbolically *offered Jesus as a living sacrifice to God, dedicating Him once and for all to the Father*. He was their great offering. They were committed to their decision and would never back away from their promise. This was their public promise to raise Jesus according to the Scriptures and teach Him to serve God and God's people as a priority in life.

The example of Joseph and Mary dedicating Jesus to the Lord is very important for Christian parents to take to heart and put into practice. Now more than ever, moms and dads need to dedicate their children to God and make their own personal commitment that they will raise their kids according to God's Word with the goal of helping them develop a vibrant, firsthand relationship with Jesus. If your children are connected with the Lord relationally, everything else will fall into place.

We Are To Dedicate Ourselves to God Daily

What's interesting about Jesus being "presented" to the Lord in Luke 2:22 is that the apostle Paul used the same Greek word when he instructed us to "present" ourselves to God. In Romans 12:1, he wrote, "I beseech you therefore, brethren, by the mercies of God, that ye *present* your bodies a living sacrifice, holy, acceptable unto God, which is your reasonable service." When Paul says to "present" (*paristemi*) your body, he's urging each of us to officially *dedicate ourselves once and for all* to the plans and purposes of God. This means we *surrender* and *place ourselves at God's disposal as a living sacrifice*.

The need for this dedication is made clear by Paul's words, "I beseech you." The word "beseech" is the Greek word *parakaleo,* and it pictures *one who comes alongside someone else or a group, as close as he can get, and passionately calls out, pleads, beckons, or begs them to do something.* It means *to beseech a person, group,* or *God to do something on one's behalf.* It can also describe *a word of prayer.*

So when Paul wrote, "I beseech you therefore, brethren," he is literally drawing as near as he can to anyone reading this passage — including us — and passionately calling out with an urgent request. The sense of pleading here is so strong that one expositor says it is a picture of the apostle Paul dropping to his knees, calling out to us, begging and pleading with us to present our bodies as a living sacrifice.

Something else remarkable about this word *parakaleo* — translated here as "beseech" — is that it is also a military term, *signifying a call to combat.* It was used in the ancient Greek world to describe commanding officers who came alongside their troops just before they went into battle. With a sense of urgency, the commander would "beseech" them, saying, "The battle you're about to enter may be very difficult, but you need to face it bravely and decide you can handle it. So, hold your head high, throw your shoulders back, stand up straight, and look the enemy in the eye as you bravely move forward into the fight."

The reason Paul also used this word "beseech" was because he knew that when you make a decision to dedicate your body to God, it will likely be a struggle with your flesh. Even Jesus experienced this wrestling match with His own flesh when He was in the Garden of Gethsemane. He struggled with accepting what God had asked Him to do. Nevertheless, Jesus did conquer His flesh through the power of the Holy Spirit (*see* Hebrews 9:14). He came to the point where He said, "...Not my will, but thine, be done" (Luke 22:42). Realize that if Jesus fought with His flesh, you will too. But through the power of His Holy Spirit, you can present yourself to God as a living sacrifice just as He did!

Your Body, Mind, and Emotions Are To Be Surrendered to the Lord

Looking once more at Romans 12:1, it says, "I beseech you therefore, brethren, by the mercies of God, that ye present your bodies a living sacrifice...." Paul's language in this verse is peculiar because prior to this writing, there had never been a *living* sacrifice — sacrifices were always dead. So, the concept of a living sacrifice is new.

To be a *living sacrifice* means God wants us to lay ourselves on the altar — which is symbolically the Cross of Christ — and stay on the altar of our own free will. We are to be completely surrendered to him — 24 hours a day, 7 days a week — in the same way that Mary and Joseph presented Jesus to the Father that day in the temple.

Notice that Paul said we are to present our "bodies." In the context of this verse, the word "bodies" involves our physical body as well as all the faculties of our soul — which is our *mind, will*, and *emotions*. Stop and think. Have you ever come to a moment in your life when you officially "presented" your body and your soul to the Lord?

Your Body

Unfortunately, there are many believers who have given their hearts to God but not their bodies. Yet, this is what God calls us to do. The Bible says, "Do you not know that your *body* is the temple (the very sanctuary) of the Holy Spirit Who lives in you, Whom you have received [as a Gift] from God? You are not your own" (1 Corinthians 6:19 *AMPC*). Friend, *your body is the very home of God's Spirit.* The question is: Does He feel welcome and at home in you?

It's not hard to tell if you have truly dedicated your body to the Lord. All you have to do is stand in front of a mirror and see what kind of shape you're in. Although we all encounter challenges and changes as we age, we can still do our best — with the help of the Holy Spirit — to be mindful of what we're eating and include some type of regular exercise and activity in our lives. The bottom line: "…Whether you eat or drink, or whatever you do, do all to the glory of God" (1 Corinthians 10:31 *NKJV*).

If you've never officially surrendered your body to the Lord, you can do so now by praying a prayer like this: "Lord, I'm giving You my body — it's Yours and no longer mine. My physical person is at Your disposal once and for all. In Jesus' name."

Your Mind

Like the body, the *mind* is another area that many Christians have never officially surrendered to God. They have given Him their heart, but their thinking remains in their own control. Some even believe they have the right to think whatever they want to think, but that's not what God says. He says, "And thou shalt love the Lord thy God with all thine heart, and with all thy soul [*mind*], and with all thy might" (Deuteronomy 6:5). So, dedicating our mind to the Lord is not a suggestion; it is a command.

Why does God want you to dedicate your mind to Him? Because *the mind is the control center of your life*, and Proverbs 23:7 confirms this. It says as a man "…thinketh in his heart, so is he…." Whoever controls your mind ultimately controls everything about you — what you do, what you say, and what you believe.

How about you? Have you ever dedicated your mind to God? You can do so by simply praying a prayer like this: "Lord, I choose to give You my mind as a living sacrifice — it's Yours and no longer mine. My memory banks and thinking capacity are at Your disposal once and for all. In Jesus' name."

Your Emotions

This brings us to the area of *emotions*. If you think about it, emotions are quite powerful, but they are also very unpredictable. You can feel several different ways about the same thing, all in the same day. When your emotions are not under the lordship of Jesus, they can become a hideous weapon that quickly leads you in the wrong direction, making you say and do things you later regret. Proverbs 25:28 (*NKJV*) verifies this saying, "Whoever has no rule over his own spirit is like a city broken down, without walls."

So who controls your emotions? Is it you, or have you dedicated them to God? According to Romans 12:1, you are to "present" — the Greek word *paristemi* — your body, your mind, your emotions, and all that you are to the Lord *as a special offering to Him*. You are to *surrender yourself and all your faculties, placing yourself at His disposal once and for all.*

If you've never committed your emotions to the Lord, you can do so now by praying a prayer like this: "Lord, I choose to give You my emotions as a living sacrifice — my feelings are Yours and no longer mine. They are at Your disposal to bring You glory every day. In Jesus' name. Amen."

The Anatomy of a Sacrifice

In the ancient world, in both the pagan and Jewish cultures, offering a sacrifice was one of the most important acts of worship. First, it was done in public, and it was very festive and celebrated. Usually, the animal being sacrificed was decorated and its horns were painted. Next, it was then laid on the altar, and its throat was cut, effectively killing it. The animal's blood was then drained out, collected in bowls, and poured out on the altar. Finally, the animal was cut into pieces and burned on the altar.

Thus, there was no such thing as a living sacrifice — it just didn't exist. All sacrifices were dead, or they weren't a sacrifice. Death and the shedding of blood were required for a sacrifice to be made or it was not a sacrifice. If a person walked off with a living animal, then all he did was create a spectacle of himself. It wasn't a real sacrifice unless something died. This brings us to the all-important question: *What does it mean to be a living sacrifice?*

Obviously, there's no physical death involved. When God says to *present your bodies as a living sacrifice,* He is telling us to be serious about climbing onto the altar every day to present ourselves to God. In our personal prayer time, we are to symbolically place ourselves on the altar — which, again, is the Cross of Christ — and say, "God I am presenting myself to You. I fully surrender to You my body and soul — my mind, my will, and my emotions. I choose to die to what I want, what I think, and how I feel about things, and I humbly place myself at Your disposal. In Jesus' name…."

Being a living sacrifice means dying to self *every day*. It is an act of surrender and dedication of all that we are to God with the decision to never take our lives back again. If there has been no death to self, there has been no sacrifice. Once we surrender our lives fully to God, we are no longer our own. We are His. We are holy — that is, we are set apart, consecrated, and dedicated to God and to His purposes. This is what it means to be a *living sacrifice.*

Being a Living Sacrifice Is Our 'Reasonable Service'

God's Word says that presenting yourself as a living sacrifice is "…holy, acceptable unto God, which is your reasonable service" (Romans 12:1). The word "acceptable" is the Greek word *euarestos*, which means *fully agreeable, fully pleasing, and fabulous*. In other words, you are *a sacrifice that God has accepted and approved*. He thinks it is fabulous when we surrender our lives to Him each day. A sacrificed life is what He accepts, consumes, and fills with His presence.

Something else to note in this verse is the phrase "reasonable service." This is a translation of the Greek phrase *logiken latreian*. The word "service" is a form of the term *latreia*, and it depicts *the sacred service of any religious priest or of the Levitical priesthood*. Hence, it was a life-long, full-time, priestly occupation. This means serving God — and offering ourselves as a living sacrifice — is our primary, *life-long occupation*. Furthermore, the Bible says this is our "reasonable service." In other words, *it is the logical thing we are to do after all that Christ did to redeem us*.

At this point you may be thinking, *What does all this have to do with the Christmas story? What about the Magi and the star they followed? What about the gifts of gold, frankincense, and myrrh? When did Mary and Joseph flee to Egypt? And when did King Herod give orders to kill all the boys in Bethlehem under the age of two?* These are all great questions regarding events that really did take place, and we will answer them in the coming lessons. But let's learn all that we can from Joseph and Mary's example.

Just as Joseph and Mary took Jesus to Jerusalem to dedicate Him in the Temple as a baby, we as Christian parents should do our best to dedicate our children (and grandchildren) to the Lord — making a commitment to raise them according to God's Word and His ways. Likewise, let's obey God's command and begin to dedicate our body and soul to Him every day. Being a living sacrifice is fabulously pleasing to Him and the most logical thing we can do for Him after all He's done for us.

In our next lesson, we will look at the lives of Simeon and Anna — two renowned people who came to see Jesus at the Temple on His day of dedication.

STUDY QUESTIONS

Study to shew thyself approved unto God, a workman that needeth not to be ashamed, rightly dividing the word of truth.
— 2 Timothy 2:15

Romans 12:1 says to "…Present your bodies a living sacrifice, holy, acceptable unto God, which is your reasonable service." This instruction is not isolated to this one verse. Rather, it is a repeated theme presented throughout the New Testament.

1. Carefully read Romans 6:4-8 and 11-14 in a few Bible verses (including the *Living Bible*) and tell how it is related to Romans 12:1.
2. How does the passage in Romans 6 expand and clarify your understanding of Romans 12:1?
3. Write out and commit to memory Paul's powerful declaration in Galatians 2:20 and make it a part of your personal prayer each day. (Also consider First Corinthians 10:31 in the *Amplified Bible*.)

PRACTICAL APPLICATION

> But be ye doers of the word, and not hearers only,
> deceiving your own selves.
> —James 1:22

1. Have you ever presented your *body* to the Lord — surrendering it as an offering to Him, never to take it back again? In what practical ways can you honor God by taking better care of your body — the temple of His Holy Spirit (*see* 1 Corinthians 6:19)?
2. Have you ever presented your *mind* to the Lord — once and for all, never to take it back again? What specific steps can you take to honor God in your thinking and "be transformed by the renewing of your mind" (*see* Romans 12:2)?
3. Who controls your *emotions* (or feelings)? Have you ever dedicated them to God? Does He have the right to tell you what to do with your emotions? What do you sense the Holy Spirit is prompting you to do to honor God more in your emotions?

LESSON 9

TOPIC

Who Were Simeon and Anna?

SCRIPTURES

1. **Luke 2:25-33** — And, behold, there was a man in Jerusalem, whose name was Simeon; and the same man was just and devout, waiting for the consolation of Israel: and the Holy Ghost was upon him. And it was revealed unto him by the Holy Ghost, that he should not

see death, before he had seen the Lord's Christ. And he came by the Spirit into the temple: and when the parents brought in the child Jesus, to do for him after the custom of the law, then took he him up in his arms, and blessed God, and said, Lord, now lettest thou thy servant depart in peace, according to thy word. For mine eyes have seen thy salvation, which thou hast prepared before the face of all people; a light to lighten the Gentiles, and the glory of thy people Israel. And Joseph and his mother marvelled at those things which were spoken of him.

2. **Luke 2:36-38** — And there was one Anna, a prophetess, the daughter of Phanuel, of the tribe of Aser: she was of a great age, and had lived with an husband seven years from her virginity. And she was a widow of about fourscore and four years, which departed not from the temple, but served God with fastings and prayers night and day. And she coming in that instant gave thanks likewise unto the Lord, and spake of him to all them that looked for redemption in Jerusalem.

3. **2 Peter 3:3,4** — Knowing this first, that there shall come in the last days scoffers, walking after their own lusts, and saying, where is the promise of his coming....

4. **2 Peter 3:8,9** — But, beloved, be not ignorant of this one thing, that one day is with the Lord as a thousand years, and a thousand years as one day. The Lord is not slack concerning his promise, as some men count slackness; but is longsuffering to us-ward, not willing that any should perish, but that all should come to repentance.

5. **1 Thessalonians 4:16,17** — The Lord himself shall descend from heaven with a shout, with the voice of the archangel, and with the trump of God: and the dead in Christ shall rise first: then we which are alive and remain shall be caught up together with them in the clouds, to meet the Lord in the air: and so shall we ever be with the Lord.

SYNOPSIS

In Lesson 8, we looked at Jesus' dedication at the Temple and learned about how Joseph and Mary presented Him to the Lord 40 days after His birth. In the same way that they fully surrendered Jesus to God's will and His purpose, we, too, are to dedicate our lives to God every day and be a living sacrifice — exclusively set apart for His purposes and plans (*see* Romans 12:1).

Interestingly, on the same day Mary and Joseph were at the Temple presenting Jesus to the Lord, two special people who were led by the Holy Spirit showed up in that divine moment. Their names were Simeon and Anna, and they both had long believed they would see the arrival of the Messiah before they left this world. On that God-ordained day at the Temple, their hopes were fulfilled.

The emphasis of this lesson:

Simeon and Anna were deeply devoted followers of God who were filled with and led by the Holy Spirit. They were eagerly waiting for the coming of the promised Messiah and believed they would see Him before they departed from this world in death. By studying their examples, we can learn what we need to do to prepare our hearts and lives for Jesus' soon return to rapture His Church!

What Does Church History Tell Us About Simeon?

When Joseph and Mary were at the Temple dedicating Jesus, the Bible says, "And, behold, there was a man in Jerusalem, whose name was Simeon; and the same man was just and devout, waiting for the consolation of Israel: and the Holy Ghost was upon him. And it was revealed unto him by the Holy Ghost, that he should not see death, before he had seen the Lord's Christ" (Luke 2:25,26). As Luke begins to relate his story, he opens with the word "behold" — the Greek word *idou*, which describes *bewilderment*, *shock*, *amazement*, and *wonder*. The use of this word shows that he is simply shocked and amazed that this noteworthy man, Simeon, showed up on the day of Jesus' dedication.

Some well-versed with ancient Jewish writers have noted that there was indeed a man by the name of Simeon who was alive and of great note in Jerusalem. He was the son of Hillel, the founder of a major theological group, and the first to ever be given the title of Rabban — the highest title that they gave to their theological doctors. You might even say he was a celebrity-type theologian in Jerusalem.

Simeon eventually succeeded his father Hillel and became the leader of the Hillel theological group. He was honored above all others as the greatest scholar and theologian of his time, eventually becoming a leader in the Jewish Sanhedrin. The Jewish leaders at that time believed Simeon was endued with a spirit of prophecy and anointed to discern the signs of the times. According to the Scriptures, he was waiting for the consolation of Israel — that is, for the coming of the Messiah.

The nation of Israel had been harassed and oppressed by Rome for many years. The coming of the Messiah would finally be a consolation — or *bring comfort* — to the Jews. Although the Messiah was long in coming, Simeon believed He would come. In fact, he believed and prophetically declared he would see the Messiah's appearance with his own eyes before he died.

Simeon Was 'Just,' 'Devout,' and 'Waiting'

Looking again at Luke 2:25, it says, "And, behold, there was a man in Jerusalem, whose name was Simeon; and the same man was just and devout, waiting for the consolation of Israel: and the Holy Ghost was upon him."

The first word Luke used to describe Simeon is the word "just," which is the Greek word *dikaios*. It means *righteous; just; correct; upright; virtuous;* or *one who keeps the commands of God*. This was a man who truly lived by God's Word.

Second, Luke said that Simeon was "devout." This is the Greek word *eulabes*, which means *devout; pious; having respect for God;* or *God-fearing*. In addition to being "just" and "devout," Simeon was also "waiting for the consolation of Israel." In Greek, the word "waiting" is *prosdechomai*, and it *pictures a hope* or *an expectation*. It means *to embrace,* to *gladly welcome,* or *to fully and completely take something without reservation or hesitation*. By using this word, Luke lets us know that Simeon had *engaged his faith* and was earnestly looking for and anticipating the "consolation of Israel."

This brings us to the word "consolation," the Greek word *paraklesis*, which describes *comfort, encouragement, support,* or *solace*. As we noted, Israel had been occupied by and subjected to the harsh rule of the Romans. Simeon had an active expectation and anticipation that at any moment the long-awaited Messiah would appear and free the nation of Israel from Roman occupation.

The Holy Spirit Was Upon Him

Another very important characteristic assigned to Simeon was that "…the Holy Ghost was upon him" (Luke 2:25). This refers to the anointing of the

Spirit and the gift of prophecy that was "upon" his life. This word "upon" is the Greek word *epi*, which means *on* or *upon*. Hence, the Spirit of God literally rested upon Simeon, and the Jewish leaders in Jerusalem believed this. Without question, he was known to operate in a spirit of prophecy, so they held him in the highest regard.

Luke 2:26 goes on to say, "And it was revealed unto him by the Holy Ghost, that he should not see death, before he had seen the Lord's Christ." The word "revealed" here is the Greek word *chrematidzo*, which is a term for *a business transaction between two people*. This describes the interaction between God and Simeon; his relationship with the Holy Spirit was so close that they conducted a great deal of business together.

This word "revealed" can also mean *to be forewarned* or *to be divinely revealed*. It is also the word used to describe *an individual who serves as a mouthpiece of divine revelations*. And one day, as Simeon communicated with the Holy Spirit, the Holy Spirit divinely revealed to him that he would see the Messiah before he died. This revelation grew so strong in Simeon that he became God's mouthpiece and began sharing this God-given conviction with others.

Scripture says that God's promise to Simeon of seeing the Messiah had been "…revealed unto him by the Holy Ghost…" (Luke 2:26). The word "by" here is the Greek word *hupo*, which means *by*, *under*, or *under the direction, guidance, or influence* of the Holy Spirit. In other words, because Simeon was in submission to the Holy Spirit, the Spirit was revealing things to him — including the promise that he would see the "Christ" before he passed from this life.

In the very next verse, we see the Holy Spirit's intimate connection with Simeon. It says, "And he came by the Spirit into the temple…" (Luke 2:27). In this verse, the word "by" is different. It is the Greek word *en*, and in context, it means *in the Spirit* or *in the control of the Spirit*. So here we see Simeon is being supernaturally directed and controlled by the Holy Spirit and led to the Temple. This word *en* (by) reinforces the reality that Simeon was living and operating in a "Spirit-filled" life *before* the Holy Spirit had been poured out on the Day of Pentecost.

Simeon Blessed Jesus and Praised God

Luke continues his narrative by telling us, "…When the parents brought in the child Jesus, to do for him after the custom of the law, then took *he*," which is Simeon, "him [Jesus] up in his arms, and blessed God, and said, Lord, now lettest thou thy servant depart in peace, according to thy word" (Luke 2:27-29). The word "blessed" here is the Greek word *eulogeo*, which means *to bless*; *to speak good words*; *to praise*; or *to celebrate*. A blessing is always *verbally expressed*, which means a blessing without spoken words is not a blessing. Simeon took Jesus into his arms and began to verbally bless God and Jesus.

Now some people have read and mistakenly believed that Simeon was old because he said, "Lord, now lettest thou thy servant depart in peace, according to thy word" (Luke 2:29). But there is nothing in this verse, in Scripture, or in Church history to confirm that notion. In fact, we know from certain historical sources that Simeon was *not* an old man at the time of Jesus' dedication. Essentially, what Simeon was saying in this passage was, "Even if I died now at this point in my life, it would be all right because I have seen what the Lord has promised."

Simeon then prayed, "For mine eyes have seen thy salvation, which thou hast prepared before the face of all people; a light to lighten the Gentiles, and the glory of thy people Israel. And Joseph and his mother marvelled at those things which were spoken of him" (Luke 2:30-33).

The word "marveled" in verse 33 is the Greek word *thaumadzo*, which means *to wonder* or *to be at a loss of words*. It indicates the *shock*, *amazement*, and *bewilderment* of Mary and Joseph at the words they were hearing from the mouth of Simeon. Being aware of his celebrity-like status, they were simply stunned that this legendary, highly respected, prophetic theologian in the city of Jerusalem would be speaking such remarkable words over their newborn Son. Indeed, Jesus' parents were left speechless.

Who Was Anna the Prophetess?

As the words left Simeon's lips, another highly respected person entered the scene. The Bible says, "And there was one Anna, a prophetess, the daughter of Phanuel, of the tribe of Aser: she was of a great age, and had lived with an husband seven years from her virginity" (Luke 2:36). Notice the first characteristic Luke gives us about Anna is that she was a *prophetess*. This indicates yet another renowned individual through whom the Spirit of prophecy operated.

Next, the Bible tells us that Anna had been married for seven years, "And she was a widow of about fourscore and four years…" (Luke 2:37). A score of years is 20 years, so fourscore and four years is 84 years. Thus, she could have been 84 years old or, as some believe, she may have been a widow 84 years. If the latter was true, she would have been over 100 years old. Whatever the case, the point is she was older — especially for that time in history.

Luke 2:37 goes on to say, "… [She] departed not from the temple, but served God with fastings and prayers night and day." This tells us Anna lived a life of prayer and intercession and was a constant resident in the temple, which means she had living quarters somewhere on the temple premises. As a prophetess, she also instructed others in what she was hearing from the Lord, especially concerning the coming of the Messiah. Like Simeon, she believed and declared the Messiah would come soon — and with Him, He would bring redemption for Jerusalem.

Notice the words "departed not" (Luke 2:37). They are a translation of the Greek words *ouk aphistemi*, which means *to depart not* or *to not step away from*. This indicates that Anna didn't take one step away from the Temple. She was so expectant to see the Messiah that she didn't leave the grounds lest she miss the moment when He would appear. Her deep devotion to God had kept her onsite for decades on end — with "fastings and prayers night and day." The word "prayers" in Greek is the word *deesis*, which describes *a request for a concrete, specific need; a petition, usually based on rights or a legal position*. This means she prayed according to the promises of the Word of God — one of the most effective ways anyone can pray and release God's power.

The Bible goes on to say, "And she coming in that instant gave thanks likewise unto the Lord, and spake of him to all them that looked for redemption in Jerusalem" (Luke 2:38). The word "instant" — the Greek word *hora* — means *in that same hour*, and it shows how in that same hour Anna and Simeon were synchronized in the way the Holy Spirit led them into the temple. Moreover, the phrase "gave thanks" means *to verbally agree with God; to verbally confess*; or *to mutually agree*. This tells us that Anna was a woman of the Word — she was standing on Scripture and living in agreement with the Lord.

Out of her God-focused, Holy Spirit-saturated life, the Bible says, "… [She] spake of him to all them that looked for redemption in Jerusalem" (Luke 2:38). The word "looked" is again the Greek word *prosdechomai*, which pictures *a hope* or *an expectation*. This verse tells us that Anna spoke about the divine revelation of the coming Messiah to all who *embraced and gladly welcomed Him without hesitation or reservation*. Every time the Holy Spirit led her to someone *earnestly looking for and anticipating the Messiah, Anna opened her mouth and in the power of the Spirit, fanned into flames people's hopes and expectations of the coming King*. Like Simeon, Anna took one look at Jesus and immediately perceived, *"This is Him! This is the Messiah!"*

So both Anna the prophetess and Simeon the highly revered theologian were considered to be anointed of God and gifted to operate in the spirit of the prophetic. They were believing that they would see the coming of the Messiah and therefore released their faith in that direction. In time, they received what they believed!

What Can We Learn From Simeon and Anna To Be Prepared for Christ's Next Coming?

As we said at the beginning of this lesson, Simeon and Anna give us an example of *what we need to do to prepare our hearts and lives for Christ's next coming*. We need to keep watching, be expectant, and engage our faith — believing He is indeed coming. As Jesus said, we are going to receive exactly what we're believing for (*see* Matthew 9:29). The times in which we live are very unique. The apostle Peter spoke of our day saying, "Knowing this first, that there shall come in the last days scoffers, walking after their own lusts, and saying, Where is the promise of his coming…" (2 Peter 3:3,4).

In this passage, the Holy Spirit gives us specific signs we can look for to confirm whether or not we are living in the last days. Through Peter, He says, "Knowing this first," which is very important. The tense in the Greek here would better be translated, "Know this, know this, know this and never forget it." Equally significant is the word "first," which indicates what he's about to say is top priority. What does Peter want us to know and never forget? That "…there shall come in the last days scoffers…" (2 Peter 3:3).

The phrase "shall come" indicates that *something is going to be widely released* in the last days, and it's going to be released in the Church. This brings us to the word "scoffers" — the Greek word *empaidzo*, which describes *one who makes fun of another through mockery*. These individuals *disdain, scorn, and ridicule* the Word of God and mock those who stand on and put their faith in it. In the last days, scoffers will ridicule believers and say, "Where is the promise of his coming? People have been saying Jesus is coming back for 2,000 years, and He hasn't come." The Bible says when you hear people talking like that, *you'll know you're in the last days.*

Interestingly, Peter says this widespread mockery will occur in the "last days." The word "last" is the Greek word *eschatos*, which is from where we get the word *eschatology, the study of the end times.* The word *eschatos* points to *the ultimate end of a thing — the extreme end.* It was used in classical Greek literature to depict *a place the farthest away, such as the end of the earth.* It signified *the final port or last stopping off for a journey, something that is final.* The Greek text here actually says, *"the end of days."* In the *end of days,* when time can sail no farther, when we come to the last port or the very end of the age, people will begin mocking the fact that Jesus is coming again.

Jesus Is Not Slow in Returning… God Is Patiently Waiting for People To Be Saved

Peter went on to say, "But, beloved, be not ignorant of this one thing, that one day is with the Lord as a thousand years, and a thousand years as one day. The Lord is not slack concerning his promise, as some men count slackness; but is longsuffering to us-ward, not willing that any should perish, but that all should come to repentance" (2 Peter 3:8,9).

Did you notice the word "slack"? It appears twice in verse 9 and is the Greek word *bradus*, which describes *something that is tardy, slow, delayed,* or *late in time.* In the context of this verse, the Holy Spirit is telling us that *God is not slow, tardy, or delayed* regarding the promises He has made. He made them, and He will fulfill them. This "felt" delay is because God is *longsuffering* and doesn't want anyone to perish.

For the sake of those who still need to come to repentance, He is extending mercy. Yes, God could take revenge on our sin-ridden society, but He doesn't because He is exceedingly patient with those who are unsaved, and He is willing to wait for the redemption of that one last person who will repent.

Jesus will return the instant the last person who is going to be saved repents and is brought into the Kingdom. In that moment, "…The Lord himself shall descend from heaven with a shout, with the voice of the archangel, and with the trump of God: and the dead in Christ shall rise first: then we which are alive and remain shall be caught up together with them in the clouds, to meet the Lord in the air: and so shall we ever be with the Lord" (1 Thessalonians 4:16,17).

Just as Christ came at His first Advent and Simeon and Anna were eagerly awaiting His arrival, He will certainly come again. In the fullness of time, He will penetrate the stratosphere and gather His people who are fervently waiting and anticipating His return. Friend, it's time to keep watching, be expectant, and engage your faith. The signs are all around us. Jesus is coming soon!

STUDY QUESTIONS

> Study to shew thyself approved unto God, a workman that
> needeth not to be ashamed, rightly dividing the word of truth.
> — 2 Timothy 2:15

1. Out of Simeon's intimate relationship with the Holy Spirit, the coming of the Messiah was divinely revealed to him. What has Jesus promised you in John 16:13-15 as you abide in relationship with Him? (Also consider Amos 3:7 and Psalm 25:14.)
2. Has the Holy Spirit given you any specific revelations about things to come — regarding either personal situations or for believers as a whole? If so, what are they?
3. Through Peter, the Holy Spirit tells us that God is *not* slack about His promises — He's *not* tardy, slow, or delayed in fulfilling what He has said. How do Numbers 23:19 and First Kings 8:56 confirm and reinforce this claim? (Also consider Psalm 111:7; Matthew 5:18; and Luke 21:33.)

PRACTICAL APPLICATION

> But be ye doers of the word, and not hearers only,
> deceiving your own selves.
> — James 1:22

1. Simeon and Anna waited with great expectation and anticipation for the Messiah to appear during their lifetime. What can you learn from their example and put into practice as you wait for the Lord's soon return?

2. Luke 2:37 informs us that Anna offered "prayers" to God day and night. This means she stood on the promises of God's Word and included them in her prayers. What issues are you currently facing that need to be addressed with the power of God's Word? According to Isaiah 62:6 (*AMPC*), how can "…you who [are His servants and by your prayers] put the Lord in remembrance [of His promises]…"? What specific scriptures can you begin to pray to turn the tide in your situation?
3. Although it may appear that Jesus is *slow* or *tardy* in returning to earth, the "felt" delay is actually because of God's longsuffering. In His mercy, He is simply holding out for the last soul to be saved. What family members and friends do you have who are not saved? How does their need for Jesus give you a fresh appreciation for God's long-suffering and mercy? Take a moment to follow the Lord's instructions in First Timothy 2:1-4 and pray for the salvation of your loved ones.

LESSON 10

TOPIC

Who Was Herod the Great and What Was His Relevance to the Birth of Christ?

SCRIPTURES

1. **Luke 2:39** — And when they had performed all things according to the law of the Lord, they returned into Galilee, to their own city Nazareth.
2. **Matthew 2:1-12** — Now when Jesus was born in Bethlehem of Judaea in the days of Herod the king, behold, there came wise men from the east to Jerusalem, saying, Where is he that is born King of the Jews? for we have seen his star in the east, and are come to worship him. When Herod the king had heard these things, he was troubled, and all Jerusalem with him. And when he had gathered all the chief priests and scribes of the people together, he demanded of them where Christ should be born. And they said unto him, In

Bethlehem of Judaea: for thus it is written by the prophet, And thou Bethlehem, in the land of Juda, art not the least among the princes of Juda: for out of thee shall come a Governor, that shall rule my people Israel. Then Herod, when he had privily called the wise men, inquired of them diligently what time the star appeared. And he sent them to Bethlehem, and said, Go and search diligently for the young child; and when ye have found him, bring me word again, that I may come and worship him also. When they had heard the king, they departed; and, lo, the star, which they saw in the east, went before them, till it came and stood over where the young child was. When they saw the star, they rejoiced with exceeding great joy. And when they were come into the house, they saw the young child with Mary his mother, and fell down, and worshipped him: and when they had opened their treasures, they presented unto him gifts; gold, and frankincense, and myrrh. And being warned of God in a dream that they should not return to Herod, they departed into their own country another way.

SYNOPSIS

It is a well-documented fact that Herod the Great was a paranoid tyrant who lived his life driven by the constant fear that someone someday would steal his throne from him. Through strategic political maneuvering, shrewd manipulation, and brutal acts of murder, Herod maintained his position as king in Judea for more than 30 years. It was toward the end of his ruthless reign that Jesus, the Son of God, was born.

The emphasis of this lesson:

The life of Herod the Great was extremely memorable, but for all the wrong reasons. His fearful, controlling, greedy, ruthless, and sexually promiscuous attributes paint a picture of the kind of person we *don't* want to be.

Details of Jesus' Birth — Exclusive to Matthew's Gospel

As we learned in our last lesson, Joseph and Mary stayed in Bethlehem after Jesus' birth and then went to the Temple 40 days later for His baby dedication. The Bible says, "And when they had performed all things according to the law of the Lord, they returned into Galilee, to their own city Nazareth" (Luke 2:39). Although Luke was an insightful historian and recorded many events surrounding the birth of Jesus, there were several occurrences that he didn't include, such as the visit from the wise men, the famous star in the east that they followed, and the gifts of gold, frankincense, and myrrh that they brought. Likewise, Luke did not mention the holy family's flight to Egypt or the killing of the innocent babies in Bethlehem. To read about these events — and the role of King Herod — we must turn our attention to the second chapter of Matthew's gospel where he wrote:

> **Now when Jesus was born in Bethlehem of Judaea in the days of Herod the king, behold, there came wise men [Magi] from the east to Jerusalem, saying, Where is he that is born King of the Jews? for we have seen his star in the east, and are come to worship him.**
>
> **When Herod the king had heard these things, he was troubled, and all Jerusalem with him. And when he had gathered all the chief priests and scribes of the people together, he demanded of them where Christ should be born. And they said unto him, In Bethlehem of Judaea: for thus it is written by the prophet, And thou Bethlehem, in the land of Juda, art not the least among the princes of Juda: for out of thee shall come a Governor, that shall rule my people Israel.**
>
> **Then Herod, when he had privily called the wise men, enquired of them diligently what time the star appeared. And he sent them to Bethlehem, and said, Go and search diligently for the young child; and when ye have found him, bring me word again, that I may come and worship him also.**
>
> **When they had heard the king, they departed; and, lo, the star, which they saw in the east, went before them, till it came and stood over where the young child was. When they saw the star, they rejoiced with exceeding great joy.**
>
> **And when they were come into the house, they saw the young child with Mary his mother, and fell down, and worshipped him: and when they had opened their treasures, they presented unto him gifts; gold, and frankincense, and myrrh.**

And being warned of God in a dream that they should not return to Herod, they departed into their own country another way.
— Matthew 2:1-12

What's interesting about this passage is that none of these events took place while the holy family was in Bethlehem. These things happened *after* they returned to Nazareth. The star in the east, the visit from the wise men, and the distribution of their gifts did not occur the night Jesus was born as religious tradition suggests. These events, along with King Herod's murderous rampage, took place nearly two years after Jesus' birth.

Why Are the Events of Jesus' Birth Often Depicted as All Occurring the Night He Was Born?

Have you ever wondered why all the events in Matthew's gospel often seem to get combined with the events of Luke's gospel and retold as if they had all taken place at the time of Jesus' birth? The reason this idea seems to be so prevalent is because Italian painters during the Middle Ages — who wanted to depict the whole Nativity story at once — consistently included all these events together on one canvas.

Today, through the medium of movies and videos, we have the capability of showing all the events of Jesus' birth in the correct sequence, time frame, and location. However, the dominating influence of the Italian artists lives on. In fact, the effect of their portraits is why we see Joseph with Mary as she gives birth to Jesus in a barn and why the angels, the shepherds, and the wise men are all depicted as coming to see Jesus the night of His birth.

Yes, Mary and Joseph were together in Bethlehem the night she gave birth to Jesus, and the shepherds were there too, along with several animals. But the star in the east, the Magi (wise men) meeting King Herod in Jerusalem, and their arrival and extraordinary gift-giving all took place about two years after His birth.

Unfortunately, most people's understanding of the birth of Jesus today comes from greeting cards that are also based on the same Italian painters' portraits, which only perpetuates the misconception. What we all really need is a return to the time-tested Scriptures and a closer look at the reliable historical accounts that will help us accurately determine what and when things really happened regarding Jesus' birth.

What Does History Tell Us About Herod the Great?

In addition to the Bible, there are several reliable historians who documented many details about Herod the Great. For instance, the Jewish historian Josephus tells us numerous facts about the brutal acts of King Herod. The same can be said of the great historian Strabo, who gives us very lucid details about the life of Herod the Great.

Interestingly, Herod was called "Herod the Great" even during his lifetime, which is not a common occurrence. The few, more widely known individuals in history who were called "the great" while they were living include: Ramses the Great, Cyrus the Great, Darius the Great, Alexander the Great, Herod the Great, Constantine the Great, Charlemagne the Great, Peter the Great, and Catherine the Great.

Herod the Great was born in 72 BC — about seven decades before the birth of Christ. He was born into a very distinguished family of great wealth that rose to a place of prominence during the rule of the Hasmonean dynasty. Herod's father was extremely prosperous and became an advisor to the Hasmonean Court. We're told by Josephus that when Herod was growing up in his opulent and influential home, he was tall, strong, athletic, well-educated, and an avid hunter that learned to ride horses.[1]

Herod's personal rise to power. It seems that when Julius Caesar announced that Herod's father was a Roman citizen in the year 47 BC, Herod also began to move up in the ranks and was soon appointed governor of Galilee. In 42 BC, he was appointed governor of Syria, and about two years later, in the year 40 BC, the Roman Senate appointed Herod to be the king of Judah. Shortly thereafter, Herod declared that Jerusalem would be the seat of his new capital.

Although Herod's rise to power was quite an achievement, his life soon became dominated by the fear of being overthrown and replaced by someone else. As deep paranoia set in, Herod reached a point where he began killing anyone he suspected of vying for his kingship. In fact, history documents he once executed 45 nobles at the same time. Several other famous people simply "disappeared," never to be seen again, and no one knew what happened to them.

Herod totally controlled the Jewish leaders. His first official act after becoming king of Judea was to ruthlessly slaughter the entire Jewish Sanhedrin in the city of Jerusalem. He then removed the legitimate high priest and installed his own high priest along with handpicked Sanhedrin members, who were primarily composed of his family, friends, or close associates. During his tenure, Herod appointed six high priests, none of whom actually descended from a priestly family. One high priest he chose was his brother-in-law, whom he later had killed.

This tells us that from the beginning of Herod the Great's rule to the time of Jesus, the Sanhedrin and the high priests were all illegitimate leaders — mere pawns and puppets in Herod's hands. One scholar says the Sanhedrin was the "religious mafia" that Herod used to control the city of Jerusalem. Clearly, these Jewish leaders were dominated by Herod — convening and dismissing upon his request. To say that he was a great manipulator is an understatement.

Herod was a great political manipulator who befriended many powerful people. For example, he formed alliances with Julius Caesar, Augustus Caesar, Marcus Agrippa, Mark Antony, and Cleopatra. In fact, some allege that at some point he was romantically involved with Cleopatra, which is not surprising in the least. Cleopatra slept with many governmental leaders in an attempt to make friends, keep the peace, and establish political alliances with neighboring nations. The one man with whom she fell in love was the Roman general named Mark Antony. Thus, Herod became a dear friend of Antony as well. So much so that when he constructed a fortress near the Temple Mount, he called it the Tower of Antonia, naming it in honor of Mark Antony. This was the same Mark Antony that was defeated by Octavian and who later committed suicide with Cleopatra.

Herod was a great successful builder. Everything he constructed was on a colossal scale. He built theatres, amphitheaters, hippodromes, and the legendary palace and city of Herodium, south of Jerusalem in the Judean Desert. He erected significant structures at Jericho, Hebron, and Caesarea Maritima. He also constructed the city of Masada and built what is known today as the Second Jewish Temple (Solomon built the first). Furthermore, he established massive palaces, fortification walls, and military fortresses, not to mention the construction of the Temple Mount walls and a major expansion of the Temple Mount itself. When it came to building, he truly lived up to his name — *Herod the Great*. In fact, many of the landmark sites that people come to Israel to visit today are remnants of Herod the Great's construction projects.

Herod was extremely prosperous and great in business. He improved trade routes, enlarged harbors, and created new markets for wine, dates, olive oil, asphalt, and other products such as glass, pottery, and perfume, which all prospered during his rule. Moreover, he amassed a gargantuan library and surrounded himself with individuals who could help him run the affairs of state and manage increasing resources. He was known as a great businessman who was even willing to melt his own gold and silver jewelry into bullion for trade during economic crises. He even allotted food supplies to neighboring states when they were in need in order to strengthen his power in the region.

Herod's rule was known as a time of great fear, suspicion, and slaughter. Due to multiple attempts to overthrow him, Herod was perpetually paranoid that someone would one day succeed in taking his throne. Consequently, every time he heard that a new king or a Messiah had been born, he went on a rampage and started killing people. This erratic, violent behavior deeply upset the entire city of Jerusalem. They dreaded any news of a new Messiah or a new king because they knew bloodshed was going to take place. Josephus said, "Herod was a man who was cruel to all alike and one who easily gave in to anger and was contemptuous of justice."[2] Apparently, he was so stricken with the fear of losing his throne he executed several family members including his mother-in-law and his wife's grandfather.

History reveals that Herod married 10 times, and his second wife was named Mariamne, a Hasmonean princess whom he wed to connect himself to the Hasmonean dynasty. Strangely, even though he deeply loved Mariamne, he ordered her to be executed when a rumor circulated that she was conspiring with others to take his throne. On another occasion, he killed his brother-in-law for the same suspicion. He even killed his three elder sons because he heard rumors that they were conspiring together to take his throne. It was this unthinkable slaughter of his sons that moved Augustus Caesar to say, "I would rather be Herod's pig than his son."[3] Strife was so prevalent in Herod's family that he altered his will six times during his lifetime. As great as he was in building, he was equally great in terrorizing.

How and When Did Herod Die?

As best we can ascertain, Herod died in 4 BC, which is very different than what most people think. If he died in 4 BC, then Jesus had to have been born at least two years earlier. That places Jesus' birth in the year 6 or 7 BC, not in the year 1, which is very important.

With regard to Herod's death, Josephus — the greatest Jewish historian that ever lived — wrote that he died as a result of sexual diseases he had contracted from multiple sexual escapades. He was extremely sexually promiscuous, sleeping with an unimaginable number of people. In the words of Josephus, He was literally "a slave to his passions."[4]

Indeed, Herod died a most miserable death at his palace in Jericho. Josephus and other historical sources document that Herod was consumed by worms that devoured his sex organs. His sin of lust conceived and literally brought forth death (*see* James 1:15). Ironically, this once exceedingly powerful, shrewd politician and manipulator — a man who knew how to control his people and the nations around him — could not control his own sexual instincts and appetite. And in the end, it killed him. Regarding Herod's death, Josephus wrote:

"From this time onwards Herod's malady began to spread to his whole body and his sufferings took a variety of forms. He had fever, though not a raging fever, an intolerable itching of the whole skin, continuous pains in the intestines, tumors in the feet as in dropsy, inflammation of the abdomen and gangrene of the private parts, engendering worms, in addition to asthma, with great difficulty in breathing, and convulsions in all his limbs."[5]

An interesting fact regarding Herod's death is that he feared no one would cry when he died because he was such a ruthless dictator. Therefore, he concocted a plan once he knew he was approaching death. Essentially, he said to some of his henchmen, "When you hear that I'm on my deathbed and I'm dying, gather all the Jewish princes of Israel and bring them into the Hippodrome. Corral them by whatever means necessary — arrest them and drag them there against their will. Once it has been announced that I've died, kill all the Jewish princes in the Hippodrome. If you slaughter them, their families will cry, and all of Israel will cry too." Herod was convinced that slaughtering the Jewish princes would guarantee a wave of national sorrow on the day he died.

Thankfully, when the news of Herod's death was announced, all the Jewish princes were released from the Hippodrome. Instead of mourning, there was great rejoicing and great laughter throughout the land on the day that Herod died.

That is a quick snapshot of the man called Herod the Great. In our next lesson, we're going to look at who the Magi were and how many of them actually came to see Jesus after He was born.

STUDY QUESTIONS

> Study to shew thyself approved unto God, a workman that
> needeth not to be ashamed, rightly dividing the word of truth.
> — 2 Timothy 2:15

1. Prior to this lesson, what did you know about Herod the Great?
2. What shocking new details did you learn about his ruthless leadership?
3. Herod's life illustrates a timeless truth regarding sin found in James 1:14,15 and Romans 6:23. What is this principle? (Also consider Proverbs 11:19; and Ezekiel 18:4.)

PRACTICAL APPLICATION

> But be ye doers of the word, and not hearers only,
> deceiving your own selves.
> — James 1:22

1. After hearing about the depth of Herod's paranoia, his merciless acts of violence, his uncontrollable sexual appetite, and his miserable death, what lessons can you extract from his life and apply to your own?
2. How does this overview of Herod's life help you better understand the cultural and political climate Jesus was born into and endured during His life? Specifically, how does it help you grasp the probable condition of the Jewish spiritual leadership (i.e. the Sanhedrin and high priest) during Jesus' ministry?

---

[1] Josephus. *Antiquities of the Jews*.

[2] Josephus. *Antiquities of the Jews*.

[3] Macrobius. *Saturnalia.*

[4] Josephus. *Antiquities of the Jews.*

[5] Josephus. *The Wars of the Jews.*

* For more information on this subject, it is recommended that you obtain Rick Renner's book *Christmas — The Rest of the Story.*

LESSON 11

TOPIC

Who Were the Magi?

SCRIPTURES

1. **Matthew 2:1-3** — Now when Jesus was born in Bethlehem of Judaea in the days of Herod the king, behold, there came wise men from the east to Jerusalem, saying, Where is he that is born King of the Jews? for we have seen his star in the east, and are come to worship him. When Herod the king had heard these things, he was troubled, and all Jerusalem with him.

SYNOPSIS

The traditional picture of the nativity scene we see today is quite different than what took place the night Jesus was born. Of course, Mary, Joseph, and Jesus were there, and the Bethlehem shepherds were also present. But what about the *wise men*? Were they there the night Jesus was born? Were there only three? Did they bring three small, boxed gifts? Although greeting cards and movies paint a picture of the shepherds and the wise men kneeling together before Jesus the night He was born, history reveals something different.

The emphasis of this lesson:

The wise men — or Magi — were exceedingly rich and powerful during the times of the New Testament. These "king-makers" were highly respected and reverently feared by all — even by kings. The fact that they searched diligently and came to worship Jesus and bring Him gifts is absolutely amazing.

Who Were the Magi?

Our story of the Magi begins in Matthew 2:1, which says, "Now when Jesus was born in Bethlehem of Judaea in the days of Herod the king, behold, there came wise men from the east to Jerusalem." The word "behold" in this verse is the Greek word *idou*, which is a term used frequently throughout the New Testament. We've noted that it carries the idea of *bewilderment, shock, amazement, and wonder*. As Matthew was recalling the birth of Jesus years after the event took place, he was still filled with *wonder* and *amazement* over what happened. It is as if he was saying, "Wow! Can you imagine it? When Jesus was born, wise men from the East showed up in Jerusalem!"

In the *King James Version*, the visitors are called "wise men," which is a translation of the Greek word *magos* — the plural form of *magi*. Herodotus, a Greek historian, noted that the Magi were *a special cast of sacred leaders for the Medes that provided priests for Persia*.[1] It seems they were gifted in the study of astronomy and were strongly influenced by Daniel who served in Babylon many centuries earlier. Although they were not kings, Tertullian noted that "[they were] "well-nigh kings" [in many respects]."[2]

Indeed, Magi were an elite, powerful, fabulously wealthy group of high-ranking priests who were devoted to interpreting dreams and who gained an international reputation for being experts at studying the constellations, which was regarded as a science at that time. A combination of scientists, politicians, and religious leaders, they were staggeringly wealthy, and they possessed so much power and political clout that, if they chose to do so, and if they, as a group, agreed to it, they had the ability to depose a king with a single word. Or with a single word, they could install a new king of their preference in the place of the one they deposed. For this reason, they were viewed as *king-makers* in Eastern lands, and without their endorsement, it would have been difficult for anyone to become or to remain a king. Interestingly, Magi were so powerful we do not have an equivalent authority for them in the world today.

Nero and Herod Both Had Close Calls With Magi

History documents that there was a rendezvous between the Magi and Emperor Nero when another emperor wanted to come to Rome to pay homage to Nero. Accompanying this outside emperor were Magi.

Although Nero was delighted that another king was coming to pay homage to him, he was deeply puzzled and terrified when he heard that Magi were traveling with him.

Knowing the tremendous influence of the Magi and that they could create serious problems for his reign and for Rome, Nero rolled out the red carpet for them, offering great accommodations and entertainment the entire time they were there. To be clear, this is the same ruthless Nero who was afraid of no one and killed anyone he wished. As the Magi left, he loaded them down with extravagant gifts with value beyond imagination. Once they departed, he threw a party in the city of Rome, celebrating the fact that nothing dreadful happened during the Magi's visit.

When Magi entered the city of Jerusalem looking for the newborn King (Jesus), Herod reacted in much the same way Nero did. In fact, he had never forgotten that in 39 BC, certain Magi were in support of a coup to depose him. *Why are these Magi coming here, and what do they want?* Herod must have asked himself as the huge caravan of travelers made its way into the city of Jerusalem. He knew these magistrates were powerful and could depose him with a single word and install someone else in his place. Frightened of what their intentions were and what their visit might bring, Herod welcomed these mighty and wise men from the East with great pomp and celebration.

What Does History Tell Us About the Magi?

Although Mark, Luke, and John are silent about the Magi, Matthew includes helpful information about them. The biblical connection with the Magi dates to the time of Daniel more than 600 years before Christ's birth. Daniel served under Kings Nebuchadnezzar and Belshazzar of Babylon and Kings Darius and Cyrus of the Medes and Persians. When Daniel was taken into captivity to Babylon in about 600 BC, many scholars believe he became the head of the Magi, and as such his prophecies and writings were not only well-known but also considered sacred by Magi for centuries.

Clearly, Daniel was highly proficient at interpreting dreams and visions and hearing from God, and as a result, his influence was felt in Babylon for centuries even after his death. Although Babylon was a pagan empire, Daniel possessed such a godly influence that the Eastern Magi revered Daniel's faith, his prophecies, and the Scriptures he treasured. He had spoken and written many prophecies regarding the future, including the coming of a great world leader that would be born in Israel. This, of course, was the long-awaited Messiah, the King of the Jews. The Magi believed — and were waiting and looking — for this world leader that Daniel had prophesied to be born.

Interestingly, in the years leading up to Christ's birth, there was a widespread belief throughout the Roman Empire that a new world leader, unlike any leader before him, was about to be born and usher in a new golden age. Even the pagan world sensed and wrote concerning a powerful deliverer that was about to emerge on the scene, and that belief was due primarily to the writings of Daniel and other prophecies he had shared. This clearly demonstrates how God can use a man (or woman) that is devoted to Him even in their service to ungodly people.

The Magi Came From the 'East'

The Bible clearly states that the wise men — or Magi — came "from the *east* to Jerusalem" (*see* Matthew 2:1). The Greek in this verse literally says they came *from the place of the rising of the sun*, and in earliest history, this could refer to ancient Media, Persia, Assyria, or Babylon. All these regions had Magi like the ones that we're discussing.

Ancient commentators give various opinions about where the Magi came from. For example, St. Maximus and Theodotus of Ancyra suggest the Magi came from *Babylon*.[3,4] Clement of Alexandria and Herodotus assert the Magi came from *Persia*.[5,6] Justin, Tertullian, and Epiphanius all propose that the Magi came from *Arabia*.[7,8,9] If we calculate the route required from each of these locations, we find all of them would have required that the Magi travel through the Syrian desert to Damascus, then southward along the sea of Galilee until they finally reached Jerusalem. And from each of these locations, it would have meant they traveled 1,000 to 1,200 miles. To travel such a distance with a massive caravan would have required at least 3 to 12 months.

The fact that these Magi were from the East meant they clearly understood that you were to treat great people greatly. They would never have shown up to visit a king empty-handed. Therefore, they needed time to prepare and fashion an extensive catalog of fabulous, magnificent gifts for this newly born world leader. When we combine the travel time and the time needed to prepare their gifts, we know that the Magi arrived in

Jerusalem nearly two full years after the birth of Christ. This means when the Magi finally appeared, Jesus was no longer a babe — He was a *toddler*. They were looking for a toddler king.

How Many Magi Were There?

Another question that is often asked is how many wise men showed up to see Jesus. Although the Bible doesn't tell us the specific number, some early Christian writers say there were *twelve* Magi that came to Jerusalem in search of Jesus, while others say there were *three*. The number three is likely based on the inference of the three gifts — gold, frankincense, and myrrh — that are mentioned in Scripture.

It's likely you've seen a picture or movie where three lonely kings show up at a stable, each one carrying a small box: one with gold, one with frankincense, and one with myrrh. But this is not accurate. Magi would never have shown up with just three measly gifts to present to the newborn King of kings. On the contrary, the inventory of gifts they were hauling would have been enormous.

Interestingly, one early Seventh Century document suggests that there were three Magi, and their names were Gaspar, Melchior, and Balthasar. Early frescos (wall paintings) actually show Gaspar as the oldest of the three — possibly about 60 years of age, European-looking, with a white beard, and the one who gave a gift of gold. Melchior is shown as a middle-aged man of about 40 years of age, Persian-looking, and the Magi who gave a gift of frankincense. Balthasar is shown as a young man of about 20 years of age, Ethiopian-looking, and the one who gave a gift of myrrh. Of course, these are very interesting traditions, but they're impossible to verify. The truth is we don't know how many Magi showed up or what their names were. Nevertheless, Matthew's gospel says they came, so we know their visit did take place.

How Did the Magi Travel?

Do you remember hearing the song "We Three Kings"? It opened with the words, "We three kings of orient are bearing gifts we traverse afar." This song tends to paint a picture of three well-to-do men wearing heavy cloaks and head wrappings, traveling across the desert alone on camelback with small gifts tucked in their minimal baggage. But is that an accurate image? Is that really how Magi traveled?

The truth is, this imagery is as ridiculously inaccurate as the president of a great nation riding a bicycle across the country by himself to visit another high-ranking official. It's just not something that happens.

History reveals that Magi traveled in a huge caravan with hundreds of servants to manage their cargo and provisions as well as to care for their animals. Also, along for the journey were many highly trained bodyguards and an army to protect the Magi through hostile territories. Again, these were powerful, highly influential individuals who were on a mission — in this case, to see and welcome the greatest ruler the world had ever known.

If there were three Magi, there would have been several hundred servants, soldiers, and bodyguards to accompany them and their cargo, which contained a plethora of extravagant treasures for the Christ-child. If there were 12 Magi, there were likely a thousand or more servants, bodyguards, and army personnel traveling with them to ensure their safety on their long journey and assist in carrying all the amazing gifts for the newborn King of kings.

Again, when Magi traveled, they did so in massive and luxurious caravans. They were regal, impressive, and the upper crust in the Eastern lands, and were treated lavishly. The coaches they were often transported in were very plush and carried on long poles by servants. These coaches were draped on every side with lavishly decorated, luxuriant materials to protect them from the weather elements of sun and wind.

When they traveled long distances, they may have dressed less formally. But before the Magi entered the city of Jerusalem where starstruck people would have filled the streets to see them, they would have exchanged their travel clothes for garments made of exotic materials and intricate weaves indicative of Eastern lands. Likewise, they would have also adorned themselves with jewels that were intended to exhibit their power and vast wealth. That's just a little insight that we know for sure about Magi.

The Magi Came To 'Worship the King'

Matthew 2:2 informs us that when the Magi entered Jerusalem, they were "saying, Where is he that is born King of the Jews? for we have seen his star in the east, and are come to worship him." Clearly, their arrival created quite a stir. Everyone — including Herod — heard that they were approaching the city, and it is likely they knew of their visit long before they actually arrived.

Interestingly, the word "saying" in this verse is a translation of the Greek word *legontes*, and the verb tense indicates ongoing activity. Thus, a better translation here would be that as the wise men entered Jerusalem, they kept on *saying and saying and saying*, "Where is He that is born King of the Jews?" As they rode up and down the streets in all the different districts of the city, the people heard these powerful "king-makers" *asking and asking and asking* for the whereabouts of the newborn King.

The word "King" is also important. It is the Greek word *basileus*, which describes *a king*, an *emperor*, or *the highest ruler*. In this case, it is capitalized in the Greek just as it is in English, which denotes it is *the greatest and highest King to ever be born*.

The Magi kept asking and asking where the King was so that they could "worship" Him. This word "worship" is the Greek word *proskuneo*, which means *to kiss the ground when prostrating before a superior*. It carries the idea of *falling down and prostrating oneself*, to *adore on one's knees*; or *to worship with all necessary physical gestures of worship*. Worship was in the hearts and on the minds of these wise men. Their intention was to find the prophesied King of all kings and bow themselves to the ground before Him in worship and adoration.

What About the Star?

Note that the Magi said, "…For we have seen his star in the east, and are come to worship him" (Matthew 2:2). Keep in mind that the Magi were experts in studying the constellations, and because of Daniel's prophecies that a world leader would be born in the future, they believed that when this particular star appeared in the heavens, it was the confirming sign for which they had been waiting.

The star has been immortalized in Christmas songs, paintings, movies, and greeting cards for 2,000 years. Many people even place a star on the top of their Christmas tree. For hundreds of years, astronomers and historians have been trying to determine exactly which star this was.

German scientist, mathematician, and natural philosopher Johannes Kepler proposed that what the Magi saw was an alignment of Jupiter and Saturn recorded in 7 BC, which was about the same time when Jesus was born.[10] This alignment of Jupiter, Saturn, and the moon took place in the constellation of Aries while Venus and Mars were in neighboring constellations. Interestingly, it would've produced a powerful, much brighter than usual, star in the night sky that would have been visible throughout the Roman Empire at that time.

Something else fascinating is that Jupiter is known as the "king" planet, as it is the largest of all planets in our solar system. It is also of great significance because it was associated with royalty. Thus, this alignment would have been perceived by the Magi as an announcement of the arrival of the long-anticipated world leader.

Although some have suggested that the dazzling display the Magi saw was a comet, there's no record of a comet at that time. Others have advocated that the Magi saw a *stella nova*, which is a star that increases and decreases in magnitude over time. Still others have said that they saw a supernova, but they could have never seen a supernova — not even with the assistance of a telescope. All these suppositions prove incorrect because they don't fit Matthew's account.

The Bible says, "…And, lo, the star which they saw in the east, went before them, till it came and stood over where the young child was" (Matthew 2:9). Thus, the star led them and guided them to where Jesus was, which is not something a star would naturally do. This magnificent sign in the night sky seems to have been a supernatural display of God.

When the Scripture says the Magi had "seen His star in the east," the word "seen" is a Greek word that means *to delightfully view, to scrutinizingly look at*, or *to behold with the intent to examine*. That is exactly what the Magi did. When they saw the star, they delightfully viewed it in the night sky again and again and again — taking a careful, scrutinizing look and examining it from all angles to fully understand its implications. Once these experts studied this dazzling display, they then made their conclusion: it was, indeed, THE SIGN that the world leader Daniel had prophesied about had finally been born.

Isn't it amazing that these mighty Magi came to worship Jesus! These king-makers were acknowledging the young Christ Child as the world leader — the King of kings — for whom they had been waiting. Due to Daniel's prophecies and what they saw in the constellations — and a figuring of dates fixed on what Daniel wrote and what other scriptures said — they knew it was time for the King of kings to be born. That is when the star appeared to announce Jesus' birth.

The Bible says, "When Herod the king had heard these things, he was troubled, and all Jerusalem with him" (Matthew 2:3). So why was Herod — and all of Jerusalem — so upset? How did he handle the arrival of these Magi from the East? That will be our focus in our next lesson.

STUDY QUESTIONS

> Study to shew thyself approved unto God, a workman that needeth not to be ashamed, rightly dividing the word of truth.
> — 2 Timothy 2:15

1. Before beginning this lesson, what did you know and believe about the wise men and their involvement in the birth of Jesus? How many did you think came, and what kind of gifts did you think they brought? In what ways has your understanding been expanded?
2. How are the prophecies recorded in Isaiah 60:3 and Daniel 7:14 fulfilled in the actions of the Magi? (Also consider Psalm 22:27-29.)
3. Without question, the wise men traveled many miles for many days and spent a great deal of money to search out and find Jesus. To what lengths are you willing to go and search out and experience the presence of Jesus? As you answer, consider the stories of a blind man named Bartimaeus (Mark 10:46-52) and a woman with a deathly bleeding issue (Mark 5:24-34).

PRACTICAL APPLICATION

> But be ye doers of the word, and not hearers only, deceiving your own selves.
> —James 1:22

1. As Matthew recalled the story of Jesus' birth years after it took place, he was still *shocked, amazed,* and *bewildered* by its retelling. What experience have you had with Jesus that still leaves you *astonished* and in *awe* of who He is?
2. The Magi were exceedingly rich and powerful people who influenced the masses by a single word of wisdom that fell from their lips. Knowing their weighty position and the fact that they sought out Jesus to *worship* Him, what does it say to you about their character? How does their example motivate you in your worship of Jesus?

[1] Herodotus. *The Histories*.

[2] Tertullian. *Against Marcion*.

[3] Maximus. *Sermon xviii on Epiphany*.

[4] Theodotus. *Sermon on the Nativity*.

[5] Clement of Alexandria. *Stromata*.

[6] Herodotus. *The Histories*.

[7] Justin Martyr. *Dialogue with Trypho*.

[8] Tertullian. *An Answer to the Jews*.

[9] Epiphanius. *Expositio Fidei [A Deposit of Faith]*.

[10] Roy B. Zuck, *Precious in His Sight: Childhood and Children in the Bible* (Eugene, OR; Wipf and Stock Publishers, 1996), p. 186.

* For more information on this subject, it is recommended that you obtain Rick Renner's book *Christmas — The Rest of the Story*.

LESSON 12

TOPIC

Why Was Herod Troubled by the News of Jesus?

SCRIPTURES

1. **Matthew 2:1-9,11** — Now when Jesus was born in Bethlehem of Judaea in the days of Herod the king, behold, there came wise men from the east to Jerusalem, saying, Where is he that is born King of the Jews? for we have seen his star in the east, and are come to worship him. When Herod the king had heard these things, he was troubled, and all Jerusalem with him. And when he had gathered all the chief priests and scribes of the people together, he demanded of them where Christ should be born. And they said unto him, In Bethlehem of Judaea: for thus it is written by the prophet, And thou Bethlehem, in the land of Juda, art not the least among the princes of Juda: for out of thee shall come a Governor, that shall rule my people Israel. Then Herod, when he had privily called the wise men, inquired of them

diligently what time the star appeared. And he sent them to Bethlehem, and said, Go and search diligently for the young child; and when ye have found him, bring me word again, that I may come and worship him also. When they had heard the king, they departed; and, lo, the star, which they saw in the east, went before them, till it came and stood over where the young child was. …And when they were come into the house, they saw the young child with Mary his mother, and fell down, and worshipped him: and when they had opened their treasures, they presented unto him gifts; gold, and frankincense, and myrrh.

2. **Luke 2:39** — And when they had performed all things according to the law of the Lord, they returned into Galilee, to their own city Nazareth.

SYNOPSIS

Herod was a principal player in the story of Jesus, and he reigned as the king of Judea from 37 BC till about 4 BC. The Bible says, "Now when Jesus was born in Bethlehem of Judaea in the days of Herod the king, behold, there came wise men from the east to Jerusalem" (Matthew 2:1). As we saw in the previous lesson, the word "behold" is the Greek word *idou*, and it carries the idea of *shock*, *bewilderment*, amazement, and *wonder*. When Matthew was recalling and recording the beginning of Jesus' life, he was still *dumbfounded* at the fact that "wise men" — the Greek word *magoi*, or Magi — from the East had traveled such a long way to get a momentary glimpse of the One called the Christ.

Remember, Magi were a sacred cast of the Medes that were very powerful, fabulously wealthy, high-ranking priests, who were devoted to interpreting dreams and studying the constellations. They had so much influence and political clout that if they agreed as a group to do so, with a single word, they could depose a king and install a new king of their preference in his place. Thus, every king in the East trembled at the sight of Magi — including King Herod the Great.

The emphasis of this lesson:

The Magi's news of the birth of the King of the Jews sent shockwaves all through Jerusalem. Herod's deep-seated fears of being dethroned drove him to order the extermination of every child in Bethlehem two years

old and under. His murderous rampage is what the people of Jerusalem feared. Miraculously, God delivered Jesus from Herod's wrath.

The Magi Were Searching for the King of All Kings

The Bible says that when the Magi came riding into Jerusalem, they were "Saying, Where is he that is born King of the Jews…" (Matthew 2:2). We saw that the word "saying" in Greek is *legontes*, and its tense here indicates that they were *saying and saying and saying* or *asking and asking and asking*, "Where is he that is born King of the Jews? Can anybody tell us? Does anyone know where the King of the Jews has been born?"

The word "King" is the Greek word *basileus*, which means *king, highest ruler*, or *emperor*. In this verse, it is capitalized in the Greek, which indicates that the Magi were in search of *the greatest King of all kings, the Ruler of all rulers, the Emperor of all emperors* — a world leader so great that even the heavens had announced His birth! This is whom the Magi believed they would find as they journeyed the long distance through the barren and rugged terrain. Their purpose was clear: they had come to "worship" the new king.

Herod and All of Jerusalem Were 'Troubled'

Scripture says, "When Herod the king had heard these things, he was troubled, and all Jerusalem with him" (Matthew 2:3). The word "troubled" here is the Greek word *tarasso*, and it means *to be agitated, shaken up, or deeply troubled*. It depicts *an emotional upheaval from getting stirred up about something*. It pictures *one so stirred up about something that he's become deeply bothered, distraught, on edge,* and *even tormented*. Thus, Herod was *agitated, shaken up*, and *in an emotional upheaval* over the news of Jesus' arrival.

When Herod heard that the Magi were making their way through the streets of Jerusalem repeatedly saying, "Where is he that is born King of the Jews," he began spiraling down into an emotional tailspin. These were Magi — king-makers. With one word they could dethrone him and enthrone another in his place. So, while he hated the fact that they were in Jerusalem, he knew he had to roll out the red carpet and treat them like royalty.

Not only was Herod troubled, but also "…all Jerusalem with him" (Matthew 2:3). The word "all" is the Greek word *pasa*, and it means *all*;

the whole; or *every single part*. It is the picture of *totality* — each and every person, no exception. In other words, *all* of Jerusalem — *every single part of the entire city* — was deeply disturbed, restless, and shaken up by the news of the birth of the King of the Jews. And the reason everyone was upset is that they knew from past experience that every time news of a new king or rival to the throne came, King Herod went on a killing rampage and began slaughtering innocent people in Jerusalem.

On the one hand, the citizens of the city would have been starstruck by these Magi coming into their town. No doubt, they would have packed the streets of Jerusalem in order to get a glimpse of these brilliant and dazzling individuals. But on the other hand, when the Magi began saying, "Where is he that is born King of the Jews," they knew that life-threatening trouble was about to erupt once the Magi left the city.

Remember, from the beginning of Herod's reign, he lived in constant fear that a day would come when a coup would succeed against him or that a rival king would supplant him and take his throne. His rule had been riddled by continual conspiracies, civil disturbances, internal plots, international plots, and counterplots. Thus, Herod used trials, scourging, imprisonments, and the slaughter of many innocent people to get information about rival kings and plots against him. Based on their experience, the residents of Jerusalem knew exactly how Herod was going to respond to the announcement that a rival king had been born.

The Magi Were Accompanied by an Army

Keep in mind, these Magi were not a group of three lone men on camels. Records show us that when Magi traveled, they did so in a huge caravan. They were so rich and politically powerful that they usually were accompanied by hundreds — in some cases over a thousand — servants, and among those traveling with them were the best military units available. These included troops that were reputed to be the best archers of the day, who used long-range bows and carried quivers of arrows and swords. They had proven time and time again that they could win even against Roman forces. In fact, in previous battles, these warriors had famously killed 10,000 Roman soldiers.

It seems that the kind of army the Magi showed up with used a succession of waves of archers on horseback that galloped near the enemy and then released a deadly hail of arrows. Each wave of warriors was quickly followed by another wave that drew near to the enemy and fired another round. Again and again, wave after wave of galloping archers released a continuous rain of arrows that annihilated their enemies.

But this was just the beginning. As the Magi military forces saw their enemies melt in fear, a final wave of horse-riding archers would advance and move in for the kill. These soldiers were dressed in invincible chain-mail suits, and each carried a long lance. As they rode toward the enemy on massive, armor-covered horses, they were a powerful force that was nearly impossible to defeat.

Are you getting the picture? When these Magi from the East showed up in Jerusalem, they came with an army! Just imagine it — a huge caravan of servants with a colossal catalog of lavish gifts, along with hundreds of highly-trained bodyguards and armed soldiers on horseback entering the city of Jerusalem, *asking* and *asking* and *asking*, "…Where is he that is born King of the Jews? for we have seen his star in the east, and are come to worship him" (Matthew 2:2).

Is it any wonder Herod and all of Jerusalem were so upset when they arrived? Remember, Herod never forgot his earlier rendezvous with Magi in 39 BC when they united in a coup and tried to depose him. In this case, he knew these mighty influential men had come to worship the newborn King, which was proof that this King — unlike him — was legitimate.

Herod had been appointed king of Judea by the Roman Senate, but this newborn King of the Jews had been prophesied for centuries, and the heavens themselves joined in recognizing Him as King. If a legitimate king had indeed been born, he would rise and take the throne of Judea, which meant Herod would no longer be in power. Hence, he was thrown into a fit of fear.

Still, he was not in any position to be rude to the Magi. So, he rolled out the red carpet and treated them like royalty. But while he was entertaining them, he was also working a plan to get information from them. Once he found out what he needed to know, he would send them on their way back home. He would then focus his efforts on locating and destroying the child they had come to worship.

Herod Interrogated the Chief Priests and Scribes

Driven by intense paranoia, Herod called an emergency meeting. The Bible says, "And when he had gathered all the chief priests and scribes of the people together, he demanded of them where Christ should be born" (Matthew 2:4). The word "demanded" in this verse is the Greek word *punthanomai*, which means *to ask, inquire,* or *to ascertain by inquiry*. It can also mean *to investigate*, and it pictures *an intense inquiry*.

When King Herod gathered the chief priests and scribes, he vigorously grilled them with questions. "Tell me exactly how, when, and where the 'Christ' was to be born," he demanded. Through intense interrogation, he sought to ascertain and pinpoint the location of Jesus' birth so that he could kill Him just as he had killed every potential competitor or rival before Him.

In a heightened state of panic, the Jewish leaders began to pull out all their holy scrolls, searching feverishly for the information Herod requested. They flipped through page after page and moved from one parchment to another until they found the exact location where Christ was to be born.

"And they [the priests and scribes] said unto him, In Bethlehem of Judaea: for thus it is written by the prophet, And thou Bethlehem, in the land of Juda, art not the least among the princes of Juda: for out of thee shall come a Governor, that shall rule my people Israel" (Matthew 2:5,6).

Herod Then Questioned the Magi

Once Herod retrieved the prophesied location of Bethlehem, he turned his attention to the Magi. He needed specific information regarding when and in what constellation the "star" first appeared that announced the Christ Child's birth. He knew if he could determine this, he could determine the age of the child. The Bible says, "Then Herod, when he had privily called the wise men, inquired of them diligently what time the star appeared" (Matthew 2:7).

First, notice that Herod conducted his interrogation of the Magi *privately*. Why? Because if the people knew he was so concerned about this newborn king that he was interviewing the Magi, they would likely begin to say, "Wow! Maybe this time a Messiah really has been born!" So, to avoid adding any possible credence or drawing attention to the situation, Herod pulled the Magi aside privately.

Next, note that the Scripture says Herod "inquired of them diligently." This phrase is from the Greek word *akriboo*, which describes *extreme accuracy, down to the finest detail, factually precise*. It pictures *exact information with the highest level of accuracy resulting from a probing investigation*. This tells us that as Herod was conducting his analytical probe, he was asking the wise men for *extreme, precise accuracy* in their answers, *down to the finest detail*.

Specifically, he asked them "…what time the star appeared" (Matthew 2:7). The word "time" is the Greek word *chronos*, which describes *time* or *chronology*. Here, it has a definite article in front of it, which indicates that Herod wanted to know *THE timeline* of events, including when "the star appeared." The word "appeared" means *to become visible*. Herod knew that the appearance of the star announced the birth of Christ, and if he could determine when it was first seen, he could better estimate the Child's age. All these details were sought after by Herod to track down Jesus' whereabouts.

Jesus Was Born About Two Years Before the Magi's Visit

From Herod's investigation, it was determined that Christ had been born about two years earlier. St. Epiphanius of Salamis (c 310-320 – 403 AD) wrote, "The Magi reached Jerusalem two full years after Jesus' birth in Bethlehem."[1] This tells us that when the Magi showed up, they were not looking for a newborn baby — they were looking for a toddler King. This fact is supported by what Luke wrote in his account: "And when they [Joseph and Mary] had performed all things according to the law of the Lord, they returned into Galilee, to their own city Nazareth" (Luke 2:39).

Forty days after Jesus' birth, He was dedicated at the Temple in Jerusalem and Mary's purification was accomplished, and then the holy family returned to their home in Nazareth. Hence, when the Magi showed up nearly two years after Jesus' birth, He was no longer in Bethlehem but in Nazareth. All Herod knew was that Christ was to be born in Bethlehem, so that is where he sent the Magi.

Matthew 2:8 says, "And he [Herod] sent them to Bethlehem, and said, Go and search diligently for the young child; and when ye have found him, bring me word again, that I may come and worship him also." The word "search" here is the Greek word *exetadzo*, and *it pictures an intense examination* or *a precise, meticulous search*.

Herod told the Magi to search "diligently," which is the Greek word *akribos*, the same word we saw in verse 7. It means *extreme accuracy; very accurate; down to the finest detail; factually precise*. It pictures *exact information with the highest level of accuracy*. Thus, what Herod had done in his probing investigation of the chief priests and scribes, he was ordering the Magi to do in their search for Christ. If necessary, they were to go from house to house until they found the exact child they were looking for.

God Redirected the Magi to Nazareth

The Bible goes on to say, "When they [the Magi] had heard the king, they departed; and, lo, the star, which they saw in the east, went before them, till it came and stood over where the young child was" (Matthew 2:9). Once more, we see the word "lo," the Greek word *idou*, which indicates *shock*, *wonder*, and sheer *amazement*. Shortly after leaving Herod's chambers, the wise men headed in the direction of Bethlehem, but they were astounded and surprised to see the star suddenly appear again.

Although Herod had sent them to Bethlehem, God intervened and redirected them with the star to where Jesus was — Nazareth. This demonstrates how people will sometimes tell us to go one way, but then God will mercifully redirect us in the right way. Indeed, as we lean on Him, trust Him, and acknowledge Him in all our decisions, He has promised to direct our steps (*see* Proverbs 3:5,6).

Amazingly, the star that had led the Magi over 1,000 miles seemed to miraculously reappear, and it "…went before them, till it came and stood over where the young child was" (Matthew 2:9). Where was Jesus? At His *house* in Nazareth. Matthew 2:11 confirms this, saying, "And when they were come into the *house*, they saw the young child with Mary his mother, and fell down, and worshipped him…." In Greek, a definite article is included, indicating *THE house* where the holy family was living.

What's interesting is that in Nazareth today, there is a wonderful place called the Sisters of Nazareth Convent, and recently, they have discovered that underneath this convent is a Byzantine church, which was constructed on top of a First Century house. According to Early Church records, that house is said to be the house of the holy family where Jesus grew up and transitioned into manhood.

Whether or not this is true, we are not certain. Nevertheless, the fact is Joseph, Mary, and Jesus were living in a house in Nazareth and no longer in the cave in Bethlehem. Two years had passed, and the Magi were supernaturally led to the home where Jesus — the toddler King — was living.

Again, Scripture says, "And when they [the Magi] were come into the *house*, they saw the young child with Mary his mother, and fell down, and worshipped him: and when they had opened their treasures, they presented unto him gifts; gold, and frankincense, and myrrh" (Matthew 2:11). What exactly do we know about these gifts the Magi brought? What were they and what was their value? That will be our focus in the next lesson.

STUDY QUESTIONS

> Study to shew thyself approved unto God, a workman that needeth not to be ashamed, rightly dividing the word of truth.
> — 2 Timothy 2:15

1. Fear is a terrible counselor, and Herod's life is a clear example. If you listen to fear, it will cause you to say and do things that can be devastating to you and others. What do these verses say about fear coming against you? What should be your attitude toward it — with God helping you?

    - 2 Timothy 1:6,7
    - Isaiah 12:2; 41:10-13; 43:1-3
    - Matthew 10:29-30
    - Hebrews 13:5,6; Proverbs 29:25; Psalm 118:5-8

2. Herod sent the Magi in the wrong direction, but God mercifully intervened and redirected them in the right way. What does God's Word say about Him directing *you* in the way you should go? What is your part in receiving His direction? Check out Psalm 25:8,9,12; 32:8; 48:14; 73:24; Proverbs 3:5-8; Isaiah 30:21; 42:16.

PRACTICAL APPLICATION

> But be ye doers of the word, and not hearers only,
> deceiving your own selves.
> — James 1:22

1. One of the most remarkable and misunderstood elements of the Christmas story is the visit of the wise men (Magi) from the East. What new facts have you discovered so far about these extraordinary men? What is your reaction to learning that hundreds of servants — and an army — regularly traveled with them? How does this change the way you see the Magi?

2. King Herod's fears drastically affected many people's lives. Have you ever been in a situation where someone else's fears adversely affected you? Has someone else's paranoia tried to "kill" the promises of God in your life? If so, what happened, and how did God faithfully bring you through it?

3. Is there anything in your life that you are so fearful of losing that it has caused you to say and do things — even ungodly things — that you deeply regret? If so, take time now to repent for giving place to fear. Ask God to forgive you and to give you the grace to trust Him and not take matters into your own hands.

---

[1] Epiphanius. *Against the Heresies.*

* For more information on this subject, it is recommended that you obtain Rick Renner's book *Christmas — The Rest of the Story*.

LESSON 13

TOPIC
What Was the Value of the Magi's Gifts?

SCRIPTURES
1. **Matthew 2:9-12** — When they had heard the king, they departed; and, lo, the star, which they saw in the east, went before them, till it came and stood over where the young child was. When they saw the star, they rejoiced with exceeding great joy. And when they were come into the house, they saw the young child with Mary his mother, and fell down, and worshipped him: and when they had opened their treasures, they presented unto him gifts; gold, and frankincense and myrrh. And being warned of God in a dream that they should not return to Herod, they departed into their own country another way.

SYNOPSIS
As we've noted in previous lessons, the Magi came from the Far East — most likely from Babylon. They had seen an extraordinary star in their night sky and believed it was *the sign* that the greatest leader the world has ever known had been born. To celebrate the birth of this King of all kings, the Magi traveled a great distance and brought very special gifts with which to honor Him. But what were those gifts really like? Were they three tiny, boxed presents of gold, frankincense, and myrrh? Or were they something else — something greater and more extravagant than you could ever imagine?

The emphasis of this lesson:

When the Magi found Jesus, they worshipped Him and presented Him with a storehouse of treasures. The massive inventory of extraordinary gifts they brought required a caravan of servants to help carry them. Historical records document that the catalog of treasures the Magi presented to Jesus would have been enormous and worth a considerable fortune!

A Quick Review of the Magi and Their Interaction With Herod

Turning our attention once again to Matthew's account of the events surrounding Jesus' birth, it says, "Now when Jesus was born in Bethlehem of Judaea in the days of Herod the king, behold, there came wise men from the east to Jerusalem" (Matthew 2:1).

We have established that these "wise men"— or Magi — were not three lonely kings traveling alone on camels across the desert. Rather, they were a group of highly influential and exceedingly rich "king-makers" accompanied by hundreds — and perhaps over a thousand — servants to assist them on their journey.

In addition to the many individuals who helped carry the needed supplies, cargo, and the gifts the Magi were bringing to the King, there were also well-trained bodyguards and an army of highly skilled archers on horseback who provided protection for the Magi.

HEROD PANICKED WHEN THE MAGI CAME

The Bible tells us that as the Magi entered Jerusalem, they were "saying, Where is he that is born King of the Jews? for we have seen his star in the east, and are come to worship him" (Matthew 2:2). But their entrance into the city was not a happy event. Matthew 2:3 continues, "When Herod the king had heard these things, he was troubled, and all Jerusalem with him." The arrival of the Magi sent Herod into a tailspin of terror for two reasons:

- **First, he knew the Magi had the power to depose him as king and install someone else in his place.**

- **Second, the Magi were announcing that a new king — the King of the Jews — had just been born.**

Suddenly, the fear that had terrorized his soul since the moment he took office was staring him in the face again, and the people of Jerusalem were just as emotionally distraught because they knew from past experience that when rumors of a new king reached Herod, he flew into a murderous rage.

HEROD RESORTED TO TACTICS OF INTERROGATION

To deal with the situation, Herod called an emergency meeting of all the top Jewish leaders. "And when he had gathered all the chief priests and scribes of the people together, he demanded of them where Christ should be born. And they said unto him, In Bethlehem of Judaea: for thus it is written by the prophet, And thou Bethlehem, in the land of Juda, art not the least among the princes of Juda: for out of thee shall come a Governor, that shall rule my people Israel" (Matthew 2:4-6).

After Herod interrogated the chief priests and scribes and learned that Bethlehem was the prophesied location of the King's birth, he privately called the Magi into his chambers and began to question them regarding the exact time the star had appeared which announced the Child's birth. Once Herod determined the timeline of when the star first appeared, he was able to determine the time of Christ's birth and ultimately His current age, which he discovered to be about two years old.

THE STAR REAPPEARED AND REDIRECTED THE MAGI

Immediately, the Bible says, "…[Herod] sent them [the Magi] to Bethlehem, and said, Go and search diligently for the young child; and when ye have found him, bring me word again, that I may come and worship him also. When they had heard the king, they departed; and, lo, the star, which they saw in the east, went before them, till it came and stood over where the young child was" (Matthew 2:8,9).

We've noted that the word "lo" in verse 9 is the Greek word *idou*, which describes shock, *wonder*, and *amazement*. When the Magi began to make their way toward Bethlehem, suddenly the star that had led them for months on end suddenly reappeared in the sky. The Bible says, "When they saw the star, they rejoiced with exceeding great joy" (Matthew 2:10). Although Herod had directed the Magi to Bethlehem, God used this supernatural sign in the night sky once more to redirect them to where Jesus was — Nazareth.

THE MAGI FOUND JESUS AT HIS HOME IN NAZARETH

"And when they were come into the *house*, they saw the young child with Mary his mother, and fell down, and worshipped him…" (Matthew 2:11). We noted in our previous lesson that today in Nazareth, there is a wonderful place called the Sisters of Nazareth Convent, which is constructed on top of a Byzantine church. Early Byzantine writings record that this church had been built there because it was the site of Jesus' childhood home. Interestingly, recent excavations reveal that there are, indeed, remains of a First Century house beneath the Byzantine church, and according to Early Church records, that house is said to be the house of the holy family where Jesus grew up and transitioned into manhood.

Whether or not this is the early childhood house of Jesus referred to in Matthew 2:11 is uncertain. What we do know is that the holy family was living in a house in Nazareth and no longer in the cave in Bethlehem where Jesus was born. By the time the Magi saw Christ, He was about two years old.

7 SIGNIFICANT POINTS SEEN IN THE MAGI'S VISIT WITH JESUS

Matthew 2:11 says, "And when they were come into the house, they saw the young child with Mary his mother, and fell down, and worshipped him: and when they had opened their treasures, they presented unto him gifts; gold, and frankincense and myrrh." In this passage, there are seven very significant things to point out:

1: The Magi entered into a "house" in Nazareth, not a cave in Bethlehem. Two years had passed since Jesus' birth, and He was no longer an infant but a toddler.

2: The Magi saw the "young child" with Mary, His mother. The words "young child" are a translation of the Greek word *paidion*, which describes *a young child in training*. This is very different than the description of Jesus in Luke 2:12. There, the angel of the Lord called Him a "babe," which is the Greek word *brephos*, meaning *a newborn infant only a few hours old*.

This is important to understand as it lets us know that when Herod sent the wise men to Bethlehem to find Jesus, He was no longer an infant; He was a *paidion* — *a young child in training*. He was a toddler learning how to walk and talk. Thus, when the Magi left Herod to continue their search, they were looking for a young child — not a newborn baby.

3: The Magi "fell down and worshiped" Him. The reason they fell down is because the long-awaited prophecy was fulfilled right before their eyes. What they and the world had been waiting for from the time of Daniel was now a reality. They had seen the cosmic sign of His coming in the sky overhead nearly two years earlier. In response, they meticulously prepared a massive catalog of gifts and made the long, arduous journey from the East into the land of Judea. The star led them to a house in Nazareth, and when their eyes fell upon Jesus, all the strength drained out of them.

The words "fell down" in Greek means they literally *collapsed* in Christ's presence, and then they worshiped Him. In Greek, the word "worship" is *proskuneo*, and it means *to kiss the ground when prostrating before a superior or to fall down and prostrate oneself*. It depicts one *adoring on one's knees and worshiping with all necessary physical gestures of worship*.

Can you imagine what must have been going through the minds of Mary and Joseph when they saw these grown men — these highly influential and powerful Magi — falling on their knees and kissing the ground in front of their two-year-old son?

4. The Magi "opened" their treasures. The word "opened" is the Greek word *anoigo*, and it means *to make way or to give entrance*. It describes *a grand and magnificent opening*. Hence, this was not the opening of three small gifts of gold, frankincense, and myrrh, which are usually pictured on greeting cards and as many have imagined.

5. The Magi "presented" Jesus with treasures and gifts. The word "presented" is the Greek word *prosphero*, and it is a compound of the word *pros*, meaning *toward*, and the word *phereo*, meaning t*o physically carry*. When these two words are compounded to form the word *prosphero*, it means *to physically carry toward*. The gifts given by the Magi were large and numerous and had to be carried into the house. Thus, the word "presented" depicts the servants of the Magi physically carrying and transporting large treasures of all kinds into the house.

6. The "treasures and gifts" they carried were numerous. The word "treasures" is the Greek word *thesauros*, meaning *a storehouse of treasures* or *cargo filled with treasure*. It is plural, indicating there were *many treasures* — just like the word "gifts," which is plural, indicating *many gifts*. The use of the words *prosphero* and *thesauros* — translated here as "presented" and "treasures" — confirms that these were not three little gifts, but rather large and numerous, extravagant treasures. They literally carried a storehouse of treasures and gave them to the young Christ-child.

7. The Magi specifically gave Jesus gifts of "gold, frankincense, and myrrh." *Gold* is plural in Greek, indicating *many gifts of gold*, which was the gift for kings. *Frankincense* was extremely rare and expensive and known as the favorite fragrance of kings. *Myrrh* was used for embalming the dead and was a prophetic gift symbolically pointing to Jesus' atoning death.

What Kinds of Gifts Were Magi Known To Give Kings?

There has been much research done on the type of gifts Magi presented to kings in the ancient world, which helps us have an accurate assessment of the quality and quantity of what the Magi likely gave to Jesus. The size of diplomatic gifts that were given to a king was always given according to the status of that king. If the king was deemed to be a *low-level* king, the Magi would bring *lesser* gifts. But if a king was deemed to be a *high-level* king, the Magi would bring *gifts of greater value*.

In the case of the Magi that came to see Jesus, they had waited for centuries for the greatest, most preeminent world leader ever to be born. So, when the constellations announced His birth, the Magi knew they needed to bring outstanding gifts that were fit for *the greatest leader ever born*. Only the finest treasures and gifts would be fitting for a king with such a status. They knew that anything less would be viewed as a diplomatic snub, which is why they took many months to prepare the vast catalog of treasures and gifts to present to Him.

The record of diplomatic gifts given in the ancient world would have included: vases, urns, plates, carpets, all kinds of clothing, and all kinds of items fashioned from gold, silver, and other rare and expensive materials. Remember, these were wealthy Magi from the East, and in the East, they lived lavishly and treated their leaders ostentatiously. People in the East traded in precious metals, gems, rugs, spices, silks, incense, and the most treasured gifts that were known in the ancient world. The massive inventory of gifts the Magi brought Jesus required a caravan of people to carry them all. To be clear, this was not three little boxes of gold, frankincense, and myrrh.

Some of the earliest texts from the ancient world that have survived recorded the kinds of gifts that were given in such a diplomatic exchange. These would have included gold and silver, ceremonial weapons, luxurious foods, animals, along with other extravagant and splendid items. Normally, Magi would present a king at their birth large quantities of gold, silver, ebony, ivory, lapis lazuli, fabulous garments spun with golden threads, exotic perfumes, and gums from rare trees and plants. Historical documents show that it was normal to give 20 talents of gold, which is 1,336 pounds of gold for a *low-level* king. But for a *high-level* king, the amount of gold would need to be greater to correspond with his greater status.

Other examples of diplomatic exchanges include beds carved from ebony and overlaid with gold, chairs overlaid with gold, footstools fashioned of ebony and ivory and overlaid with gold, and other items made of gold or inlaid with gold. Goblets, jewelry, clothes, perfume containers, boats, knives, figurines, gold-covered chariots, and thrones were all customary gifts. Moreover, dignitaries were also endowed with bronze, alabaster, malachite, various other creations either made with or inlaid with semi-precious stones, linen, cloths of the finest materials known at that time, more garments, and as many as a thousand jars of "sweet oils" from the East along with nearly limitless gifts made of ivory and stone.

Gold, Frankincense, and Myrrh Were Very Costly

Looking once again at Matthew 2:11, it says, "…[The Magi] presented unto him [Jesus] gifts; gold, and frankincense, and myrrh." The word **"gold"** here is the Greek word *chrusos*, which describes *profound wealth* and depicts *the purest form of gold*. Although there were lesser forms that were mixed with other metals, *chrusos* was the highest quality of gold available. It was the kind that was reserved for the wealthy, for nobility, and for those that were politically powerful. This was the same "gold" that dignitaries and kings used to make their cups, bowls, plates, saucers, platters, and many other items. Furthermore, items made from *chrusos* (gold) were the kind that ambassadors or heads of state would have brought to another king. That is what they brought to Jesus.

The Bible also says that Jesus was given **"frankincense."** This word is from the Greek word *libanos*, which is *the word for the frankincense tree and the gum derived from it*. Frankincense was a very hard item to obtain because it didn't grow in Israel; it grew in Arabia and Sheba and had to be imported quite a long distance. This made it very expensive, and because it was so expensive and difficult to fabricate, it was primarily used in the Temple worship in Jerusalem. Scholars estimate about 700 pounds of it were used annually. It produced a powerful fragrance when it was burned and was the favorite fragrance of kings. Thus, you would only give frankincense to a real king.

The third substance presented to Jesus by the Magi was **"myrrh."** In Greek, the word "myrrh" is *smurna*, and it describes *a bitter gum and costly perfume which exudes from a certain tree or shrub in Arabia and Ethiopia*. It was primarily used as *an antiseptic and as an ointment for embalming the dead*. It was also used to help alleviate headaches. This was a very strange gift to give to a child. But the fact that it was used for embalming the dead makes it a prophetic gift that was symbolic of Jesus' death.

Each Was Prophetically Symbolic

When you take each of these gifts into account, they have great significance. Gold was a gift for a *king*. Frankincense was connected with a *priest* and his priestly functions. And myrrh was a component in perfume used for embalming the bodies of those who had died. Thus, it symbolically prophesied of His death as our *Savior*. He was born to be the Messiah — the Lamb of God that would take away the sins of the world. These three gifts of the Magi prophetically foretold that Jesus would eventually serve in the role of *King, High Priest*, and *Savior* of mankind through His death and resurrection.

The estimated value of all the Magi's gifts for Jesus was extraordinary! In keeping with the records of Eastern customs, a *low-level king* in those days that was visited by Magi — or by a head of state — would customarily receive 1,336 pounds of gold. By today's standards, that has a monetary value of multiple millions of dollars. Again, that was a gift for a low-level king.

Jesus was *not* — and is not — a low-level king. He is the King of all kings! Accordingly, He was presented with gifts and treasures corresponding with His status. Not only was Jesus given gold, but also frankincense and myrrh, which were even more valuable than gold because of their rarity. Can you imagine the monetary value of all those gifts combined? The catalog of treasures the Magi brought would have been enormous and worth a considerable fortune! Think about it: If the stars in the cosmos were announcing His birth — if they stood still to show where the King of kings was born — can you imagine the immensity of the gifts He was presented? The value is simply mind-boggling!

What Ever Became of the Magi?

After presenting all their gifts and treasures to Jesus, the Bible says the Magi, "…being warned of God in a dream that they should not return to Herod, they departed into their own country another way" (Matthew 2:12). Notice that God used a dream to warn them of the danger of returning to Herod. Part of the Magi's job was to interpret dreams. Hence, God spoke to them in the language they understood, which is exactly what He'll do for you.

Now, you may be wondering, *What happened to the Magi? They played such a major role in Jesus' life, what became of them?* One early document traced to an Aryan writer in the Sixth Century states, "When the apostle Thomas was on his way to India to preach, he stopped and presented the full story of the Cross and the resurrection to the Magi. They believed Thomas, and they were baptized."[1]

Another ancient account says that Helena, who was the mother of the emperor Constantine, later recovered the bodies of the Magi and put them into beautiful, ornamented caskets and ordered their remains to be placed at the St. Hagia Sophia Church in Constantinople. Some scholars suggest that the relics of the Magi were removed to Milan and then later, in 1163 AD, moved to Cologne, Germany. Interestingly, today at the cathedral in Cologne, there are large, gilded sarcophaguses behind the high altar that supposedly contains the relics of the Magi. These coffins were even opened at one time displaying actual skeletons.

Are these caskets the actual remains of the original Magi that Helena recovered? Did the apostle Thomas lead the Magi to Christ and then baptize them? It is impossible to verify these claims. Nevertheless, whether or not these caskets are those of the real Magi, we can trust that God would make sure that these wise men would have heard the full story of the Gospel and given them ample opportunity to repent and give their lives to Jesus (*see* Titus 2:11).

In our next lesson, we will take a close look at the holy family's flight to Egypt and King Herod's response to his request being disregarded by the Magi.

STUDY QUESTIONS

> Study to shew thyself approved unto God, a workman that
> needeth not to be ashamed, rightly dividing the word of truth.
> — 2 Timothy 2:15

When God sent His Son Jesus to earth on a mission, He provided all the money, all the supplies, and all the people Jesus would need to help Him get the job done. As you obediently seek to do the will of God, you can trust Him to do the same in your life.

1. How do Acts 10:34 and 35; Romans 2:11 and 10:12 reassure you that God will take care of you just like He took care of Jesus? (Also consider Job 34:19 and Ephesians 6:9.)
2. What has God promised to do for you in Philippians 4:19 and Second Corinthians 9:8?
3. According to Second Corinthians 9:11-13, what is a primary reason for this promise?

PRACTICAL APPLICATION

> But be ye doers of the word, and not hearers only,
> deceiving your own selves.
> — James 1:22

Without question, this lesson was packed with a great deal of eye-opening information on the Christmas story. Let's take a few moments to unpack and jot down what we learned.

1. What new facts did you discover from the *7 significant points of the Magi's visit* with Jesus?
2. What details surprised you regarding the historical record of *diplomatic gifts given to kings*?
3. What fresh insights did you learn about the *gold, frankincense,* and *myrrh* given to Jesus?
4. What do each of these gifts prophetically declare about His life's mission?
5. How do all these facts instill a fresh sense of awe and wonder for Christ and the amazing Christmas story?

[1] Chrysostom. *On the Statues*.

* For more information on this subject, it is recommended that you obtain Rick Renner's book *Christmas — The Rest of the Story*.

LESSON 14

TOPIC
The Flight Into Egypt and the Massacre of the Innocents

SCRIPTURES
1. **Matthew 2:11-16** — And when they were come into the house, they saw the young child with Mary his mother, and fell down, and worshipped him: and when they had opened their treasures, they presented unto him gifts; gold, and frankincense and myrrh. And being warned of God in a dream that they should not return to Herod, they departed into their own country another way. And when they were departed, behold, the angel of the Lord appeareth to Joseph in a dream, saying, Arise, and take the young child and his mother, and flee into Egypt, and be thou there until I bring thee word: for Herod will seek the young child to destroy him. When he arose, he took the young child and his mother by night, and departed into Egypt, and was there until the death of Herod: that it might be fulfilled which was spoken of the Lord by the prophet, saying, Out of Egypt have I called my son. Then Herod, when he saw that he was mocked of the wise men, was exceeding wroth, and sent forth, and slew all the children that were in Bethlehem, and in all the coasts thereof, from two years old and under, according to the time which he had diligently inquired of the wise men.
2. **Philippians 4:19** — But my God shall supply all your need according to his riches in glory by Christ Jesus.
3. **Matthew 2:19-23** — But when Herod was dead, behold, an angel of the Lord appeareth in a dream to Joseph in Egypt, saying, Arise, and take the young child and his mother, and go into the land of Israel: for they are dead which sought the young child's life. And he arose, and

took the young child and his mother, and came into the land of Israel. But when he [Joseph] heard that Archelaus did reign in Judaea in the room of his father Herod, he was afraid to go thither: notwithstanding, being warned of God in a dream, he turned aside into the parts of Galilee: And he came and dwelt in a city called Nazareth: that it might be fulfilled which was spoken by the prophets, He shall be called a Nazarene.

SYNOPSIS

Matthew 2:11 says, "And when they were come into the house, they saw the young child with Mary his mother, and fell down, and worshipped him: and when they had opened their treasures, they presented unto him gifts; gold, and frankincense and myrrh." In our last lesson, we noted that the word "treasures" is the Greek word *thesauros*, meaning *a storehouse of treasures* or *cargo filled with treasure*. And because it is plural, it indicates there were *many treasures*. There were also multiple "gifts," including frankincense, myrrh, and many items made of the purest gold. The catalog of gifts the Magi gave to Jesus was enormous, and their value would have been a literal fortune.

After the Magi lavishly poured out their gifts upon Jesus, the Bible says, "And being warned of God in a dream that they should not return to Herod, they departed into their own country another way" (Matthew 2:12). This passage demonstrates that God knows how to speak to each of us in the way we understand. These Magi were professionals at interpreting dreams. Thus, God customized His message to them through a dream. They knew beyond the shadow of a doubt who had spoken to them and what they were to do.

The emphasis of this lesson:

Herod's persistent fears and suspicions of losing his throne to a rival are what fueled the fire of his recurring murderous acts, including the massacre of all the babies in Bethlehem. God protected and provided for His Son, Jesus, as well as Joseph and Mary — making a way of escape into the land of Egypt where they lived for about three years.

An Angel Issued Orders to Evacuate

The wise men weren't the only ones having dreams. Matthew 2:13 says, "And when they [the Magi] were departed, behold, the angel of the Lord appeareth to Joseph in a dream, saying, Arise, and take the young child and his mother, and flee into Egypt, and be thou there until I bring thee word: for Herod will seek the young child to destroy him."

In this passage, the word "flee" is important. It is the Greek word *pheugo*, which means *to flee* or *to take flight*. It can also mean *to run away*; *to run as fast as possible*; or *to escape*. It pictures one's feet flying as he runs from a situation. Hence, the angel in Joseph's dream told him to move his feet as fast as he could and get his family out of Nazareth and into Egypt.

Furthermore, the angel said, "…Herod will seek the young child to destroy him" (Matthew 2:13). The phrase "will seek" is the Greek word *zeteo*. Here, the tense is futuristic and means he *will pursue, will seek*, or *will earnestly search for*. In a negative sense, *it depicts one so upset about not getting what he wants and one so intent on getting his own way that he will search, seek, and investigate, never giving up in his pursuit to get what he wants*. It can also denote *a scheming individual who manipulates people, events, or circumstances to get whatever he wants*.

With this meaning in mind, we can see that Herod was not going to give up easily. In fact, he didn't plan on terminating his search until he *destroyed* the young child. The word "destroy" in this verse is the Greek word *apollumi*, which means *destroy, ruin*, or *devastate*. It pictures *total destruction*. The angel of the Lord was keenly aware of Herod's intentions, which is why he issued orders for Joseph and His family to evacuate Nazareth.

Once again, we see Joseph didn't question God. Rather, he responded in prompt obedience, which is what God is looking for from you and all His people The Bible says, "When he arose, he took the young child and his mother by night, and departed into Egypt" (Matthew 2:14).

Herod Flew Into a Murderous Rage

Time passed, and when Herod still had not heard from the Magi, the Bible says he felt "mocked" (*see* Matthew 2:16). The Greek word for "mocked" is *empaidzo*, which means t*o be outwitted*; t*o be made fun of*; *to be ridiculed*; or *to be mocked*. After treating the Magi like royalty, Herod was deeply offended that they had outwitted him and gone home another way.

Matthew 2:16 says, "…When he saw that he was mocked of the wise men, [he] was exceeding wroth…." The word "wroth" here is the Greek word *thumoo*, which describes someone who is enraged or *livid*. It pictures *uncontrollable anger*. Verse 16 goes on to say that Herod "…sent forth, and slew all the children that were in Bethlehem, and in all the coasts thereof, from two years old and under, according to the time which he had diligently enquired of the wise men." The word "slew" is the Greek word *anaireo*, which means *to take away the life of another, to slay, to kill,* or *to brutally murder*.

If you remember, Herod had conducted an intensive interrogation of the religious leaders and then questioned the wise men. He demanded to know all the details of the prophecy concerning Jesus, including the "time" when the Magi first saw the star appear. The word "time" in Greek is the word *chronos*, which describes *the chronology* or *timeline* of events. By determining when the star was first seen, he estimated the Child's age to be about two years old. This fits the meaning of the Greek word *paidion*, which is used multiple times throughout Matthew 2 and describes *a toddler*, not an infant.

In spite of all Herod was able to determine, he didn't know that Jesus and His parents had left Bethlehem after His dedication and were safely back at home in Nazareth. This shows us that Satan is not all-knowing, and he is not as smart as some people think. Clearly, he could not identify which child was the prophesied King of the Jews, which is why he sent his troops to Bethlehem to kill all the babies that were two years old and younger. In his mind, by killing them all, he was sure to destroy the newly born King.

How Many Babies Did Herod Kill?

Strangely, Matthew is the only gospel writer to record this genocide in Bethlehem. It wasn't even recorded by the Jewish historian Josephus. To understand why, we need to first recap some important details regarding King Herod and then look at what Josephus primarily documented.

Herod's order to kill all the children two years old and under in Bethlehem fits the description of the brutality he was known for. From the onset of his reign, he was extremely paranoid of any threat to his throne, and every time he got wind of a possible conspiracy, he started exterminating people — even family members. However, in the grand scheme of things, the actual number of babies and toddlers he had killed in Bethlehem didn't compare to all the other horrific deeds he had done.

Now, there are differing statistics regarding the number of babies massacred in Bethlehem. One record says Herod killed 14,000 boys, and another says he killed 64,000, which would be an atrocity. However, there is a problem with both these numbers. Bethlehem — at its largest estimate — was a village of about 480 people. Therefore, it wasn't possible for Herod to have murdered 14,000 or 64,000 infants and toddlers. Based on the actual population of Bethlehem at that time, modern scholars have estimated the number of children massacred to fewer than 20. Some historians bring the figure down to 15, while others say it was 10 or 12. There are even some that say it was only about 6 boys that were killed.

To be clear — the killing of *any* child is horrific. The point here is that the number of children killed was much smaller than most imagine, and in the light of all the atrocities Herod did in his lifetime, his brutal acts in Bethlehem were not as significant. More than likely, Josephus didn't record this event because he primarily documented the larger acts of barbarism committed by Herod during the last years of his life.

Miraculously, through all this mayhem, Jesus and His parents were protected and placed out of the reach of Herod's murderous hands. This was the result of Joseph listening to God's instructions to leave Nazareth and flee to Egypt. Joseph's close relationship with God and prompt obedience led to the saving of his whole family. In the same way, as you stay close to the Lord, listening and obeying what He says, you will live in His divine protection.

In Egypt, God Supplied the Holy Family's Every Need

There was a world of difference between Nazareth and Egypt. Nevertheless, it was a logical place for Joseph, Mary, and Jesus to find refuge because it was outside Herod's domain — they could hide more easily there. Egypt was one of the most luxurious nations on the earth at that time, but as a foreigner, Joseph would've had no legal right to work there. Equally challenging is the fact that the holy family was on the move the entire time they were there. That said, Joseph would never have had the opportunity to get a steady job.

The fact that Joseph was constantly packing up and moving his family from one location to another, and that he couldn't work, made living as foreigners in Egypt very expensive. But none of this caught God by surprise. He knew all these details in advance, which is why He supernaturally orchestrated the arrival of the Magi and the presentation of all their treasures and gifts just before prompting Joseph to leave Nazareth and go to Egypt. God supplied the financial resources to meet His Son's needs while the holy family was living life on the move.

You might say the holy family experienced the fulfillment of the Philippians 4:19 promise, which says, "But my God shall supply all your need according to his riches in glory by Christ Jesus." The word "supply" here means *to make full, to feel complete*, or *to be filled to the point of satisfaction*. It was the very word used to describe *any kind of container that was filled and packed to the point of overflowing*. The word "need" in this verse depicts *any deficit or any need that must be met*. And the word "riches" in the Greek describes *wealth so great it cannot be tabulated*.

Taking into account the original Greek meaning of these words, here is the *Renner Interpretive Version* (*RIV*) of Philippians 4:19:

> **But my God will supply your needs so completely that He will eliminate all your deficiencies. He will meet all your physical and tangible needs until you are so full you have no more capacity to hold anything else. He will supply all your needs until you are totally filled, packed full and overflowing to the point of bursting at the seams and spilling over!**

Although we don't know how much financial provision Joseph and Mary had with them while they were traveling through Egypt, we do know that God supplied all their physical and tangible needs completely and that they had no lack whatsoever.

What Happened to the Rest of the Money?

Scholars estimate that Joseph, Mary, and Jesus stayed in the land of Egypt for about three years and traveled more than 1,200 miles on foot, by animal, and by ship. Although we know that they used a portion of the fortune presented to Jesus by the Magi to live on, there is no way they could carry all the gifts and treasures with them everywhere they went on their journey. So where did the rest of all the money and resources go?

We believe the answer to this question is found in the fabulous city of Sepphoris, which was about four or five miles from Nazareth. If you remember, Sepphoris was the big, beautiful, bustling city that Herod Agrippa had chosen to be his capital. Known as the "Ornament of Galilee," it also served as the banking center of the Middle East. Since it was the city where Joseph worked and had built a reputation as a skilled technician, it is likely that all the funds and treasures were deposited there.

When Joseph died, Jesus' great uncle was given the guardianship of Him and His family and all its resources. Believe it or not, this uncle that Jesus and His family were entrusted to was a man named Joseph of Arimathea. He was the brother of Mary's father, who just happened to become the wealthiest man in Israel. Scholars believe that he likely managed these funds, which may explain why during Jesus' ministry there is no record that He ever took an offering. He always had all the money He needed to do ministry — He even had a full-time treasurer.

This means when Jesus came into Mary and Joseph's life, not only were they blessed with a little Baby Boy, but they also experienced a drastic improvement of their economic status. God the Father had sent Jesus, His Son, on a mission. And He provided all the money, all the supplies, and all the people Jesus would need to get the job done. And He will do the same for you as you walk out His divine will for your life.

The Flight *To* and *Through* Egypt

To make the journey from Judea to Egypt, the holy family could have taken one of two different routes. The first and easiest route was the well-known coastal road known as the *Via Maris*, which means "way of the sea." It made its way from Damascus down along the Sea of Galilee, through the land of Israel and along the Mediterranean Sea until it came to Egypt. It was a popular and quick way to get to Egypt.

The alternate route was less used and took its travelers through the desert. Although it was a barren wilderness and much harder to traverse, it was more secretive and probably safer for individuals, helping them avoid detection. Most scholars believe it was this alternate route that the holy family took, and the oldest records from the Egyptian Coptic Church confirm this. Even though this desert route required 14 days to reach Egypt, it would have been more difficult for Herod's spies to find them.

Once Herod realized the Christ Child had escaped, he dispatched spies into the land of Egypt to search for Him. That is why the holy family was in constant movement the entire time they were there. Hence, their flight to Egypt is traditionally called the *Flight Through Egypt*. Today, the Egyptian Coptic Church is very proud of the fact that the holy family lived in Egypt for a period of time, and from the earliest ages, they documented all the places where Joseph, Mary, and Jesus stopped while they were in flight.

Here is a condensed list of about 30 places where the holy family passed through or stayed temporarily during their time in Egypt:

- Upon first arriving in Egypt, the holy family came to the **Nile Delta** where they briefly stayed at a village about 72 miles northeast of Old Cairo.

- From there, they fled south to **Mostorod**, about seven miles from Old Cairo.

- From there, they fled temporarily to **Belbeis**.

- From there, they fled onward to **Meniet Samanoud**, where records show that the local population showed them hospitality for the time they were there.

- From there, they fled to the ancient city of **Burullus**.

- From there, they fled across the Rosetta branch of the Nile River to **Wadi el-Natroun**, which is in the western desert of Egypt. When Egyptian Christianity later began to flourish, monasteries were built in this region as a tribute to the holy family's short-term stay there.

- From there, they fled south across the Eastern bank of the Nile River to the cities of **Matareyah** and **Ain Shams**.

- From there, they fled to the famous Egyptian ancient city of **Heliopolis**.

- From Heliopolis, they fled to **Old Cairo**, where they would have seen the Sphinx, the Pyramids of Giza, and other Egyptian monuments.

- From there, they fled again to **Maady**, which was a city that in pharaonic times was a district of Memphis, the ancient capital of Egypt.

- While in Maady, Coptic Church documents show that Joseph befriended sailors who worked on boats and ships that floated on the Nile River. Due to his friendship with them, soon the holy family fled by ship south via the Nile River to *Deir El-Garnous* and to *Ashnein El-Nasara*.

- From there, they fled by the Nile River to *Bahnassa*. Though we do not know how long they stayed there, Bahnassa was so associated with the holy family that later it was called the Egyptian hometown of Jesus.

- From there, they fled to *Samalout*.

- From Samalout, they fled crossed the Nile River to the Eastern bank, where Coptic documents say they briefly stayed at *Gabal al-Tair*.

- From there, they fled along the Nile River to *Nazlet Ebeid*.

- From there, they fled south back across to the western bank of the Nile River to dwell temporarily in *Al-Ashmunein*.

- From there, they fled to *Dairout Al-Sharif* (also known by its Greek name *Philes*).

- From there, they fled to *Qussqam*.

- From there, they fled approximately seven miles to *Meir* where they found a hospitable community that welcomed them.

- From there, they fled again to *Gabal Qussqam*, an ancient city where an altar had been built to the Lord in the land of Egypt, and it seems the holy family lived there for approximately six months.

Without question, what the angel had said about Herod *seeking diligently* to find Christ became a reality (*see* Matthew 2:13). The whole time the holy family was in Egypt, Herod pulled out all the stops, sending spies to locate Jesus and terminate His life. The Bible says the holy family "…was there until the death of Herod: that it might be fulfilled which was spoken of the Lord by the prophet, saying, Out of Egypt have I called my son" (Matthew 2:15).

The Holy Family's Return to Nazareth

The Bible goes on to say, "But when Herod was dead, behold, an angel of the Lord appeareth in a dream to Joseph in Egypt, saying, Arise, and take the young child and his mother, and go into the land of Israel: for they are dead which sought the young child's life. And he arose, and took the young child and his mother, and came into the land of Israel. But when he [Joseph] heard that Archelaus did reign in Judaea in the room of his father Herod, he was afraid to go thither: notwithstanding, being warned of God in a dream, he turned aside into the parts of Galilee: And he came and dwelt in a city called Nazareth: that it might be fulfilled which was spoken by the prophets, He shall be called a Nazarene" (Matthew 2:19-23).

Every prophetic word spoken in Scripture about Jesus was fulfilled. Even through the difficult years of being hunted and living on the run in Egypt, God faithfully provided everything Jesus and His parents needed. That is the very same thing He will do for you!

In our final lesson, we will wrap up our study by focusing on the *Real Purpose of Christmas*.

STUDY QUESTIONS

> Study to shew thyself approved unto God, a workman that
> needeth not to be ashamed, rightly dividing the word of truth.
> — 2 Timothy 2:15

On at least *four* different occasions, God spoke to and directed Joseph through divine *dreams*. You can read about these encounters in Matthew 1:20-25; 2:13-15,19-23.

1. What do you notice about God's communication to Joseph in these dreams?
2. What about Joseph's reaction to God's directions?
3. Who was impacted by Joseph's response? What blessing resulted?
4. What does his example speak to you personally? (For more on the role of dreams, consider Numbers 12:6 and Joel 2:28.)

PRACTICAL APPLICATION

> But be ye doers of the word, and not hearers only,
> deceiving your own selves.
> —James 1:22

1. More than likely, living in Egypt for three years was not on Mary and Joseph's agenda. In fact, it was probably a major *detour*. Yet, it was God's will for their family's safety. Can you remember a time in your life when God took you on an unexpected detour? How did you react? How did God use that unplanned situation to protect and better your life? What did He teach you through it?

2. One thing from this story is quite clear: Regardless of the enemy's evil schemes, God's plans and purposes will prevail and be fulfilled in your life as you trust and obey Him. Look up and write out the incredible promise of Proverbs 21:30 in the *NIV* and allow the Holy Spirit to plant it deep within your heart.

3. Dreams are one of the ways God speaks to us and directs our steps. Has the Lord ever given you a dream to direct or correct you? If so, what was it and what did He speak to you? How did you respond? Is there anything you wish you had done differently?

4. Along with dreams, God speaks to us in several other ways, such as through His Word, His Holy Spirit, and sometimes through fellow believers. One major indicator He often uses to confirm that what you're about to do or say has His approval is *giving you His peace in your spirit*. Read and write out the powerful truth of Colossians 3:15 — preferably in a translation like *The Amplified Bible* — and commit it to memory.

LESSON 15

TOPIC

The Real Purpose of Christmas

SCRIPTURES

1. **Philippians 2:8-11** — And being found in fashion as a man, he humbled himself, and became obedient unto death, even the death of the

cross. Wherefore God also hath highly exalted him, and given him a name which is above every name: that at the name of Jesus every knee should bow, of things in heaven, and things in earth, and things under the earth; and that every tongue should confess that Jesus Christ is Lord, to the glory of God the Father.

2. **John 19:28** — ...[Jesus said] I thirst....

SYNOPSIS

When we think about Christmas, we usually think about Baby Jesus being laid in a manger in Bethlehem, but when you stop to think about it, Christmas is so much more than that. As we saw in Lesson 4, when Jesus was wrapped in swaddling clothes and laid in that manger, God was proclaiming to the world from the very beginning that Jesus was the Lamb of God, born to take away the sin of the world. Thus, the real purpose of Christmas was God becoming a man of flesh and blood, living a sinless life, and dying on the Cross to pay the penalty for our sins. Through Jesus' death and resurrection, the works of the devil have been destroyed and we are given new life in Him! Friend, that is the true meaning of Christmas!

The emphasis of this lesson:

Jesus was God manifested in the form of flesh-and-blood man. The invisible Creator became visible to all of creation and humbly lived a servant's life and died a criminal's death. By this, Satan and sin were defeated, and those who put their faith in Him are redeemed.

God Was 'Fashioned' As a Man

In Lesson 5, "A Holy Moment," we learned about the miraculous incarnation of God as described by the apostle Paul in Philippians 2:6-8. Here Paul depicts the real purpose of Christmas in the clearest of terms. Speaking of Jesus, Paul wrote, "Who, being in the form of God, thought it not robbery to be equal with God: but made himself of no reputation, and took upon him the form of a servant, and was made in the likeness of men" (vs. 6,7).

Paul went on to say, "And being found in fashion as a man, he humbled himself, and became obedient unto death, even the death of the cross" (Philippians 2:8). In this verse, the word "fashion" is the old Greek word *schema*, which was borrowed from the ancient tale of a king who desperately wanted to walk and live among his people, but he couldn't because everyone would recognize him, and he would be mobbed.

It seems that day after day, the king looked out his window and watched his citizens walking on the streets of his kingdom, and he longed to be with them. Moved with compassion, he devised a plan. *I know what I'll do*, he said to himself. *I'll shed these kingly garments and put on the clothing of a commoner. I'll then go out into the streets and live among my people, and no one will recognize me.* Thus, the king did just as he said. He exchanged his royal clothing for that of an everyday citizen, slipped out of his palace and into the community, and no one recognized him because he looked like everyone else.

When the Bible says that Jesus was found in "fashion" as a man, it describes God the Father as the king in this ancient story. He loved His creation so much and longed to be among His people, but He couldn't because His attributes were too powerful for human flesh to endure. To overcome this obstacle, God took upon Himself the form of a servant. He reached into the material world, grabbed hold of flesh, and re-clothed Himself in the form of Jesus. Thus, the King of kings and Lord of lords emptied Himself of all His glorious attributes and entered the human race as a baby.

Interestingly, God looked so much like us, the Bible says, "He was in the world, and the world was made by him, and the world knew him not. He came unto his own, and his own received him not" (John 1:10,11). For 33 years He lived among us, being fully God and fully man, and then in His final days on earth, "…He humbled himself, and became obedient unto death, even the death of the cross" (Philippians 2:8).

He Humbled Himself Unto Death

To further demonstrate His love for humanity, the Bible says, "…He humbled himself, and became obedient unto death, even the death of the cross" (Philippians 2:8). The word "humbled" is the Greek word *tapeinao*, and it means *to be humble, to be lowly*, and *to be willing to stoop to any measure that is needed.* If you think it's difficult to humble yourself to accommodate someone, think about how low God willingly stooped to save you from Satan's clutches and eternal death. He emptied Himself of all His glorious attributes, left His throne in Heaven, and became obedient unto death.

This word "obedient" is powerful. It is the Greek word *hupakouo*, which is a compound of two words: the word *hupo*, meaning *to be under*, and the word *akouo*, meaning *I hear*, which is where we get the word *acoustics*. When these two words are compounded to form the word *hupakouo*, it pictures *someone who is under someone else's authority, listening to what that superior is speaking to them*. That is exactly what Jesus did. He "humbled" Himself, stooping to the lowest point possible, and became "obedient," coming under the Father's authority (*hupo*) and listening to what He said to Him (*akouo*).

Make no mistake: Jesus *despised* the Cross and the shame that came with it (*see* Hebrews 12:2). Yet, He endured the Cross and all that came with it for the *joy* of what would result — countless people like you accepting His sacrifice and being restored in relationship to God. After listening to what the Father had to say, Jesus carried out His orders and became obedient unto death, and the *King James Version* says, "…even the death of the cross" (Philippians 2:8). In Greek, the word "even" is the word *de*, and it emphatically means *EVEN!* A better translation would be, *"Can you even imagine it! Jesus stooped so low that He willingly died the miserable death on the Cross!"*

What 'Death on the Cross' Involved

In the First Century, there was no death more wretched that the death of the cross. In fact, crucifixion was so horrific that famous Roman philosopher Seneca (c. 4 BC-65 AD) said that suicide was preferable to crucifixion because crucifixion was simply so miserable.[1] In the New Testament, the word "cross" and "crucified" in Greek is *stauros*, and describes *an upright, pointed stake used for the punishment of criminals*. It was used to depict *those hung up, impaled, beheaded, and publicly displayed, and was always used in connection with public executions*. Hanging a criminal publicly was intended to bring humiliation to the accused.

Crucifixion was the lowest and most barbaric form of punishment in the ancient world. Flavius Josephus described crucifixion as the most wretched of all deaths.[2] At the time that Jesus was crucified, the act of crucifixion was entirely in the hands of Roman authorities. This punishment was reserved for the most serious offenders, usually for those who had committed some kind of treason or who had participated in or sponsored state terrorism.

The Crossbeam and the Nails

Once the offender reached the place where the crucifixion was to occur, he was laid on the crossbeam that he carried. Soldiers would then stretch the victim's arms out and drive a five-inch iron nail through each of his wrists. It was not through the palm of his hands, but through his wrists and into the cross beam.

After being nailed to the crossbeam, the victim was hoisted by a rope, and the crossbeam was dropped into a notch on the top of the upright post. When the crossbeam dropped into the groove, the victim suffered excruciating pain as his hands and wrists were wrenched by the sudden jerking motion. Eventually, the weight of the victim's body caused his arms to be pulled from their sockets.

Once the victim's wrists were secured in place on the crossbeam, the feet came next. The victim's legs would be positioned so that the feet were pointed downward with the soles pressed against the post on which he was suspended. A long nail would then be driven between the bones of the feet. The nail was lodged firmly enough between those bones to prevent it from tearing through the feet as the victim arched upward gasping for breath.

The Process of Asphyxiation

In order for the victim to breathe, he had to push himself up by the feet, which were nailed to the vertical post. Because the pressure in his feet became unbearable, it wasn't possible to remain in that position for very long. Eventually, he would collapse back into the hanging position.

As the victim pushed up and collapsed back down again and again over a long period of time, his shoulders eventually dislocated and popped out of joint. Soon afterward, the elbows and wrists would follow. Historians tell us these various dislocations caused the arms to be extended up to nine inches longer than normal, often resulting in terrible cramps in the victim's arm muscles and making it impossible for him to push himself up any longer to breathe. When he was finally too exhausted and could no longer push himself up on the nail lodged in his feet, the process of asphyxiation began.

Jesus experienced all this torture on the Cross. When He dropped down with the full weight of His body on the nails that were driven through

His wrists, it sent horrific pain up His arms that registered in His brain. Added to this torture was the agony caused by the constant grating of His back that had just been scourged. Every time He pushed Himself up to breathe and then collapsed back into a hanging position, His back grated against the upright post.

Due to the extreme loss of blood and hyperventilation, a victim would begin to experience severe dehydration. We can see this in Jesus' own crucifixion when He cried out, "I thirst" (*see* John 19:28). After several hours of this torment, the victim's heart would begin to fail. Next, his lungs would collapse, and the excess fluid would begin filling the lining of his heart and lungs, adding to the slow process of asphyxiation. A person who was crucified eventually drowned as his own fluids filled his lungs.

The Purpose in Breaking the Victim's Legs

At this point, a Roman soldier would come and check the victim's breathing to determine whether they were alive or dead. In Jesus' case, when the soldier came, he thrust his spear into Jesus' side. One expert noted that if Jesus had been alive when the soldier did this, the soldier would have heard a loud sucking sound caused by air being inhaled past the freshly made wound in the chest. But the Bible tells us explicitly that a mixture of water and blood came pouring forth from the wound the spear had made in Jesus' side, which was evidence that Jesus' heart and lungs had shut down and were now filled with fluid. It was enough to assure the soldier that Jesus was already dead.

It was customary for Roman soldiers to break the lower leg bones of a person being crucified to make it impossible for the victim to push himself upward to breathe and thus causing him to asphyxiate at a much quicker rate. However, because of the blood and the water that gushed from Jesus' side, He was already considered dead. So there was no reason for the soldier to hasten Jesus' death by breaking His legs. Hence, His legs were never broken, which was a fulfillment of Psalm 34:20.

This is a brief taste of Roman crucifixion. It is exactly what Christ experienced on the Cross. His naked body, which had been ripped to shreds by the Roman scourge and bruised from head to toe, was flaunted in humiliation before a watching world. This is the torturous death that Jesus — who was God in the flesh — humbled Himself and stooped so low to endure for you and all humanity.

Many people today like to wear a cross around their neck, in their ears, or even have it tattooed on their body. We think it's a beautiful symbol, but the fact is, the cross of Jesus Christ was a disgusting, repulsive, and nauseating sight. Yet, that's why God Almighty came to earth, took on the form of flesh in the womb of the Virgin Mary, and was born as a little infant in that cave in Bethlehem. His sole mission was to die the death on the Cross to purchase our salvation. Friend, that is the real purpose of Christmas.

Jesus Was Highly Exalted Above All Others

The Bible tells us that because Christ willingly stooped so low, God has exalted Him on high! The apostle Paul captures this in Philippians 2:9, where he said, "Wherefore God also hath highly exalted him, and given him a name which is above every name." Notice the phrase "highly exalted." It is from the Greek word *huperupsoo*, and it is only used once in the entire New Testament. It means *to make exceedingly high*, *to elevate beyond*, *to the highest place*; or *to elevate exceedingly*.

God elevated Jesus to the highest place by giving Him a "…name which is above every name." The word "name" in Greek is *onoma*, which means *name, fame*, or *reputation*. As a result of Jesus' obedience to the Father's instructions, He has been granted a *name* and *reputation* unlike anyone else! In fact, it is "above every name."

The word "above" is the Greek word *huper*, which means over, *above, and beyond*. Jesus' name depicts *something that is way beyond measure*; *it conveys the idea of superiority or something that is unsurpassed, unequaled, or unrivaled*. He has a fame and reputation above "every" name. That word "every" is the Greek word *pan*, which signifies *all*; it is *all-encompassing*. In other words, it describes *every name, nothing excluded*.

Every Knee Will Bow, Every Tongue Will Confess That Jesus Christ Is Lord!

To all this, Paul added, "That at the name of Jesus every knee should bow, of things in heaven, and things in earth, and things under the earth. And that every tongue should confess that Jesus Christ is Lord, to the glory of God the Father" (Philippians 2:10,11). Twice more, we see the word "every" — the Greek word *pan*. The use of this word indicates *every* knee and *every* tongue — *not one excluded*.

The Bible says every knee will "bow" before Jesus. This word "bow" is the Greek word *kampto*, which means *to bend the knee* or *to bow the knee in honor and respect before the ultimate authority*. It also says every "tongue should confess that Jesus Christ is Lord." In Greek, the word "confess" is *exomologeo*, which means *to declare*; *to say out loud*; *to exclaim*; to loudly confess; *to divulge or to blurt out*.

This verse declares that a day is coming when every knee of every person that has ever lived — past, present, and future — will bow in honor and respect for Jesus. This includes believers and unbelievers — those who are in Heaven and those who are in hell. And as they bow, every tongue will exclaim and declare out loud the undeniable fact that "…Jesus Christ is Lord, to the glory of God the Father" (Philippians 2:11). At some point, Heaven, earth, and hell will all resound with the thunderous acknowledgment that "Jesus is Lord," which in Greek literally means He is *Lord* or *Supreme Master*.

Christmas Is All About the Cross

If you have a family member or friend who doesn't know Jesus, why not use this season to remind them that Christmas is more than just about presents, a tree with lights, and a little baby who was laid in a manger? That Baby was born with the Cross in mind. He willingly came to die as the Lamb of God who takes away the sin of the world.

Is there any better gift you could give someone for Christmas than to tell them the Good News that Jesus paid the price for their sin, and they can be forgiven? That the authority of Satan has been broken over their lives? The Scripture says, "…For this purpose the Son of God was manifested, that He might destroy the works of the devil" (1 John 3:8 *NKJV*). That's what Christmas is all about — it's all about what Jesus did on the Cross.

So this year, in addition to talking about the Baby in the manger, talk about the magnificent Good News that God took on human flesh in the form of Jesus and was born to be the Lamb of God that takes away the sin of the world. Through the stripes of His scourging, we find healing, and through His shed blood, we have forgiveness of sin. That, friend, is the real purpose of Christmas!

STUDY QUESTIONS

> Study to shew thyself approved unto God, a workman that needeth not to be ashamed, rightly dividing the word of truth.
> — 2 Timothy 2:15

1. In this lesson, we have learned a lot about Jesus' humility and obedience. To a great degree, the lens through which He viewed every day of His life can be summed up in John 5:19 and 30. What was the essence of His life perspective?

2. On a scale of 1 to 10, how concerned are you about your *earthly* reputation (1 being not concerned at all and 10 being extremely concerned)? Using the same scale, how concerned are you about your *heavenly* reputation (pleasing the heart of God)? Consider Proverbs 29:25 and First Thessalonians 2:4.

3. According to Jesus' words in Matthew 6:19-21 and Paul's words in Colossians 3:1-3, where are you to focus your heart and mind? (Also consider Romans 12:1,2.) In what practical ways might you put these passages into practice?

4. In light of your answers, what adjustments do you feel you need to make so that your heart is more set on pleasing the heart of God? Invite the Holy Spirit to release His supernatural power in your life to cultivate a heart of obedience towards Him.

PRACTICAL APPLICATION

> But be ye doers of the word, and not hearers only, deceiving your own selves.
> — James 1:22

1. After hearing the Christmas story told through the verses of Philippians 2:6-11, what is your greatest takeaway? What aspect of His sacrifice has touched your heart most deeply in all that you've learned?

2. Before making His earthly debut in Bethlehem, Jesus eternally existed with the Father in Heaven. To fulfill God's will, He had to empty Himself of all His heavenly glory. Pause for a moment and pray: *Lord, what are You asking me to empty myself of in order for me to do Your will? What do I need to shed from my life?* Be still and listen. What is the Holy Spirit speaking to you?

3. The Bible says that Jesus was *obedient*, which means He *came under the Father's authority, listened to His words of instruction, and then carried out His orders*. In what areas of your life are you struggling to submit to the authority of God's Word? How can you surrender yourself and this situation to God? If you're not sure, tell the Lord and ask Him to show you what to do.

---

[1] Tacitus. *Annals.*

[2] Josephus. *The Wars of the Jews.*

* For more information on this subject, it is recommended that you obtain Rick Renner's book *Christmas — The Rest of the Story.*

Notes

Notes

CLAIM YOUR FREE RESOURCE!

As a way of introducing you further to the teaching ministry of Rick Renner, we would like to send you free of charge his teaching CD, "How To Receive a Miraculous Touch From God."

In His earthly ministry, Jesus commonly healed *all* who were sick of *all* their diseases. In this profound message, learn about the manifold dimensions of Christ's wisdom, goodness, power, and love toward all humanity who came to Him in faith with their needs.

☑ **YES, I want to receive Rick Renner's monthly teaching letter!**

Simply scan the QR code to claim this resource or go to: **renner.org/claim-your-free-offer**

WITH US!

 renner.org    facebook.com/rickrenner

 youtube.com/rennerministries    instagram.com/rickrrenner

www.ingramcontent.com/pod-product-compliance
Lightning Source LLC
Chambersburg PA
CBHW070457100426
42743CB00010B/1658